500 Great Places to Stay in Britain

09

G

- Coast & Country Holidays
- Full range of family accommodation

Duddings Country Cottages, Timberscombe, Dunster, Somerset (page 164)

Contents

England

Board

Self-Catering

Caravans & Camping

Scotland

Board

Self-Catering

Caravans & Camping

Wales

Board

Self-Catering

Caravans & Camping

Ireland

Self Catering

© FHG Guides Ltd, 2009
ISBN 978-1-85055-413-4

Maps: ©MAPS IN MINUTES™ / Collins Bartholomew 2007

Typeset by FHG Guides Ltd, Paisley.
Printed and bound in China by Imago.

Distribution. Book Trade: ORCA Book Services, Stanley House,
3 Fleets Lane, Poole, Dorset BH15 3AJ
(Tel: 01202 665432; Fax: 01202 666219)
e-mail: mail@orcabookservices.co.uk
Published by FHG Guides Ltd., Abbey Mill Business Centre,
Seedhill, Paisley PA1 ITJ (Tel: 0141-887 0428 Fax: 0141-889 7204).
e-mail: admin@fhguides.co.uk

500 Great Places to Stay is published by FHG Guides Ltd,
part of Kuperard Group.

Cover design: FHG Guides
Cover Picture: Canal at Newbury, photo courtesy of Berkshire Tourism

symbols

	Totally non-smoking		Pets Welcome
	Children Welcome		Short Breaks
	Suitable for Disabled Guests		Licensed

England

Board

Petwood Hotel, Woodhall Spa, Lincolnshire, page 84

Fairwater Head Hotel, near Axminster, Devon, page 17

Acton Scott Farm, Church Stretton, Shropshire, page 88

The Waterhead, Ambleside, Cumbria, page 118

England and Wales · Counties

NORTHUMBERLAND

TYNE & WEAR

DURHAM

CUMBRIA 42 41 40 39 43

ISLE OF MAN

NORTH YORKSHIRE

38 EAST RIDING OF YORKSHIRE

LANCASHIRE 34

WEST YORKSHIRE 37

33 36 35

GREATER MANCHESTER S. YORKSHIRE

32 30 31

ISLE OF ANGLESEY

CONWY b CHESHIRE DERBYSHIRE LINCOLNSHIRE

a NOTTINGHAMSHIRE

c 29 27 26

GWYNEDD STAFFORDSHIRE

28 LEICESTERSHIRE RUTLAND

25 24 NORFOLK

SHROPSHIRE WEST MIDLANDS

CEREDIGION POWYS WORCESTERSHIRE NORTHAMPTONSHIRE CAMBRIDGESHIRE SUFFOLK

WARWICKSHIRE

HEREFORDSHIRE 23 BEDFORDSHIRE

CARMARTHENSHIRE 22 ESSEX

PEMBROKESHIRE GLOUCESTERSHIRE BUCKINGHAMSHIRE HERTFORDSHIRE

l m o OXFORDSHIRE 10

d e h g k n 12 GREATER 9

f j 21 17 16 15 11 LONDON 8

i 20 19 18 14 13

WILTSHIRE

SURREY KENT

SOMERSET HAMPSHIRE

5 WEST SUSSEX EAST SUSSEX

DEVON 6 7

DORSET 3 4

ISLE OF WIGHT

CORNWALL

1 2

Unitary Authorities – England & Wales

1. Plymouth	12. Windsor & Maidenhead	23. Milton Keynes
2. Torbay	13. Bracknell Forest	24. Peterborough
3. Poole	14. Wokingham	25. Leicester
4. Bournemouth	15. Reading	26. Nottingham
5. Southampton	16. West Berkshire	27. Derby
6. Portsmouth	17. Swindon	28. Telford & Wrekin
7. Brighton & Hove	18. Bath & Northeast Somerset	29. Stoke-on-Trent
8. Medway	19. North Somerset	30. Warrington
9. Thurrock	20. Bristol	31. Halton
10. Southend	21. South Gloucestershire	32. Merseyside
11. Slough	22. Luton	33. Blackburn with Darwen

34. Blackpool
35. N.E. Lincolnshire
36. North Lincolnshire
37. Kingston-upon-Hull
38. York
39. Redcar & Cleveland
40. Middlesborough
41. Stockton-on-Tees
42. Darlington
43. Hartlepool

NORTH WALES
a. Denbighshire
b. Flintshire
c. Wrexham

SOUTH WALES
d. Swansea
e. Neath & Port Talbot
f. Bridgend
g. Rhondda Cynon Taff
h. Merthyr Tydfil
i. Vale of Glamorgan
j. Cardiff
k. Caerphilly
l. Blaenau Gwent
m. Torfaen
n. Newport
o. Monmouthshire

Cornwall

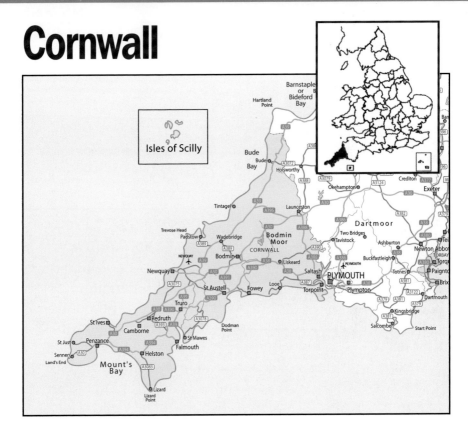

Cornwall receives most of its visitors over the summer months, exploring the beautiful beaches and indulging in the exceptional clotted cream teas - but the county has much to offer besides the Cornish pastie and the traditional bucket and spade holiday. The "shoulder" and winter months offer opportunities for the discerning visitor which may go unnoticed in the annual stampede to the beaches. There are villages boasting curious and ancient names - Come To Good, Ting Tang, London Apprentice and Indian Queens, often sporting parish churches, ancient graveyards and distinctive crosses which reveal their early Christian history. Wayside crosses, holy wells and Celtic stone circles are reminders that the Cornish are true Celts - it was they who embossed the headlands with cliff forts to repel marauders.

To discover more about life in the Iron Age there are numerous settlements to visit, for example Castle an Dinas, one of the largest preserved hill forts in Cornwall. Alternatively Chysauster Ancient Village is a deserted Roman village comprising eight well-preserved houses around an open court. More up-to-date is St Michael's Mount with its 14th century castle, or Prideaux Place, a stunning Elizabethan House, and Lanhydrock, the National Trust's most visited property in Cornwall, which was once the residence of a local family whose wealth came from tin mining.

A useful index of towns/counties appears on pages 347-350

symbols

Totally non-smoking		Pets Welcome
Children Welcome	**SB**	Short Breaks
Suitable for Disabled Guests		Licensed

Hendra Farm

Situated just off the main Helston/Falmouth road, is an ideal centre for touring Cornwall; three miles to Helston, eight to both Redruth and Falmouth. Safe sandy beaches within easy reach – five miles to the sea. Two double, one single, and one family bedrooms with washbasins and tea-making facilities; bathroom and toilets; sittingroom and two diningrooms. Cot, babysitting and reduced rates offered for children. No objection to pets. Car necessary, parking space. Open all year except Christmas. Evening Dinner optional. Tea and homemade cake before bed.

Bed and Breakfast only from £20 per night.

Mrs P. Roberts, Hendra Farm, Wendron, Helston TR13 0NR • 01326 340470

Silver
SILVER AWARD

Trewint Farm

A Cornish Cream tea awaits your arrival; enjoy the peace and tranquillity of the countryside. Trewint is a working farm, well known for its prize-winning cattle. Enjoy walks around the area, or make use of the games room. All rooms are en suite, with matching decor, and TV and tea/coffee facilities. Have breakfast overlooking the garden, and watch the birds while you enjoy the farmhouse fare. Ideal for National Trust properties; Looe six miles.
Also available: self catering properties, sleep 4/5. Ideal for winter breaks.
Bed and Breakfast £28-£35 • Self-catering from £220.

★★★★
FARMHOUSE

**Mrs Rowe, Trewint Farm, Menheniot, Liskeard PL14 3RE • 01579 347155
e-mail: holidays@trewintfarm.co.uk • www.trewintfarm.co.uk**

• Bake Farm •

**Pelynt, Looe, Cornwall PL13 2QQ
Tel: 01503 220244**

This is an old farmhouse, bearing the Trelawney Coat of Arms (1610), situated midway between Looe and Fowey. Two double and one family bedroom, all en suite and decorated to a high standard, have tea/coffee making facilities and TV. Sorry, no pets, no smoking. Open from March to October. A car is essential for touring the area, ample parking. There is much to see and do here – horse riding, coastal walks, golf, National Trust properties, the Eden Project and Heligan Gardens are within easy reach. The sea is only five miles away and there is shark fishing at Looe.

Bed and Breakfast from £27 to £30. Brochure available on request.
e-mail: bakefarm@btopenworld.com • www.bakefarm.co.uk

★★★★
GUEST
ACCOMMODATION

In a spectacular location, enjoying uninterrupted views of Looe and St George's Island, our coastal farm is a haven for the walker and birdwatcher – you can meet our Shire horses too. This beautifully decorated and furnished bungalow has three spacious en suite bedrooms, two with their own large conservatory with lovely valley views. They offer every comfort, including colour TV, central heating and beverage trays. There is ample parking, and wheelchair access if required. Savour delicious meals whilst gazing across the water, relax in the lounge or on the patio and watch the sun setting over Looe.

- Exceptional location
- Luxury rooms with sea or rural view
- 10 minute walk down to the South West Coastal Path to Millendreath Beach
- Prize winning Shire Horses
- Ample parking
- Wheelchair friendly
- No Smoking

AA
★★★★
FARMHOUSE

"Enjoy our little piece of paradise"

Lancallan is a large 17th century farmhouse on a working 700-acre dairy and beef farm in a beautiful rural setting, one mile from Mevagissey. We are close to Heligan Gardens, lovely coastal walks and sandy beaches, and are well situated for day trips throughout Cornwall. Also six to eight miles from the Eden Project (20 minutes' drive). Enjoy a traditional farmhouse breakfast in a warm and friendly atmosphere.

Accommodation comprises one twin room and two double en suite rooms (all with colour TV and tea/coffee facilities); bathroom, lounge and diningroom.

Terms and brochure available on request. SAE please.

Mrs Dawn Rundle, Lancallan Farm, Mevagissey, St Austell PL26 6EW
Tel & Fax: 01726 842284
e-mail: dawn@lancallan.fsnet.co.uk • www.lancallanfarm.co.uk

MULLION Mrs Joan Hyde, Campden House, The Commons, Mullion TR12 7HZ (01326 240365).
Campden House offers comfortable accommodation in a peaceful setting with large gardens and a beautiful sea view. It is within easy reach of Mullion, Polurrian and Poldhu Coves, and is ideally situated for exploring the beautiful coast and countryside of the Lizard. Mullion golf course is less than one mile away. All seven bedrooms have handbasin with hot and cold water and comfortable beds; some rooms are en suite. There is a large sun lounge, TV lounge with colour TV and a large dining room. Guests have access to the lounges, bedrooms and gardens at all times.
Rates: Bed and Breakfast en suite £26 pppn.
• Children and pets welcome.

SB

Take a break in the heart of Cornwall

A warm and friendly welcome awaits you at Pensalda. Situated on the main A3058 road, an ideal location from which to explore the finest coastline in Europe. Close to airport and the Eden Project. Double and family rooms available, all en suite, all with TV, tea/coffee making facilities, including two chalets set in a lovely garden.

Fire certificate • Large car park
• Licensed • Central heating
• Non-smoking.

Bed and Breakfast from £23
Special offer breaks
November to March
(excluding Christmas and New Year).

Karen and John, Pensalda Guest House, 98 Henver Road,
Newquay TR7 3BL • Tel & Fax: 01637 874601
e-mail: karen_pensalda@yahoo.co.uk
www.pensalda-guesthouse.co.uk

LONG CROSS HOTEL & VICTORIAN GARDENS

**TRELIGHTS, PORT ISAAC
PL29 3TF
Tel: 01208 880243**

Lovely Victorian country house hotel with four acres of restored gardens set in beautiful tranquil location overlooking the coast. Close to the area's best beaches, golf courses and other attractions. Spacious, comfortable interior, with newly refurbished en suite bedrooms and suites.

www.longcrosshotel.co.uk

Chilcotts

Without stepping onto a road, slip through the side gate of this 16th Century listed cottage into a landscape owned by the National Trust and designated as an Area of Outstanding Natural Beauty. Closest cottage to nearby Bossiney beach for rock pools, surfing, safe swimming and caves to explore. Walk the airy cliff path north to nearby Rocky Valley or on to picturesque Boscastle Harbour. Southwards takes you to the ruins of King Arthur's Castle and onwards to busy Trebarwith Strand. Notice you have not stepped onto a road yet? Detached traditional country cottage ideal for a small number of guests. Home cooking, warm informal atmosphere, large bright double/family bedrooms with beamed ceilings and olde worlde feel. All rooms have TV, tea/coffee makers. May I send you a brochure? *Directions: Bossiney adjoins Tintagel on the B3263 (coast road), Chilcotts adjoins large lay-by with telephone box.* **Bed and Breakfast from £20 • Self-catering annexe available.**

Cate West, Chilcotts, Bossiney, Tintagel PL34 0AY •Tel & Fax: 01840 770324 • e-mail: cwest2@toucansurf.com

---

Publisher's note

Devon

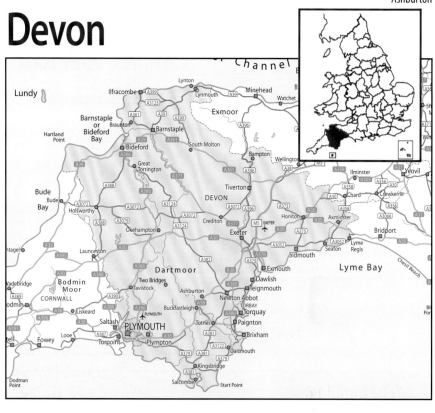

Gages Mill   Buckfastleigh Road, Ashburton TQ13 7JW

Lovely 14th century former wool mill, set in over an acre of gardens on the edge of the Dartmoor National Park. Seven delightful en suite rooms, one on the ground floor; all with tea and coffee making facilities, central heating, hairdryers, radio and alarm clocks. Large comfortable dining room with corner bar and granite archways. Cosy sitting room. Licensed. Ample car parking. Ideal base for touring South Devon or visiting Exeter, Plymouth, Dartmouth, the many National Trust properties and other places of interest. Children over 12 years welcome. Sorry no pets. Bed and Breakfast only.

Lynda Richards • Tel & Fax: 01364 652391
e-mail: gagesmill@aol.com • www.gagesmill.co.uk

Please note

All the information in this book is given in good faith in the belief that it is correct. However, the publishers cannot guarantee the facts given in these pages, neither are they responsible for changes in policy, ownership or terms that may take place after the date of going to press. Readers should always satisfy themselves that the facilities they require are available and that the terms, if quoted, still apply.

Hayne Farm

Cheriton Fitzpaine Crediton EX17 4HR

Occupied by members of the same family since the 17th Century, Hayne Farm is sited in a quiet lane with its own extensive gardens, summer house, small wood and duck pond.
It is the ideal setting for a relaxing break or holiday.

Many charming features include an oak beamed fireplace, and lounge with easy chairs and television.
3 bedrooms, two with double beds and a third en suite family room. All have tea and coffee making facilities.
Children are welcome and cot, high chair and baby sitting can be provided. No smoking or pets.

There are many places to see in the area including National Trust houses and gardens.
Exmoor and Dartmoor are within easy driving time as are the north and south Devon coasts.
The cathedral city of Exeter is a 30 minute drive away and provides shopping and entertainment.

Full cooked breakfasts are provided for guests, and local pubs are within easy reach for evening meals.
Packed lunches are available on request; evening meals by prior arrangement.

Bed & Breakfast from £25.00, reductions for children.

Mrs M Reed • Tel: 01363 866392

Welcome to our cosy farmhouse with a friendly service.
Easy level parking. Working farm. Farm walks with sea views.
Relax in our large beautiful garden, and listen to the birdsong while watching our sheep, cattle and wildlife nearby.
A real oasis yet just four miles to Dartmouth and beaches and one mile to Dartmouth Golf Club and Woodlands Leisure Park.
Three comfortable en suite double or twin rooms with all facilities.
Bed and full English breakfast (Aga cooked) from £30 per person per night. Reductions for longer stays.
Self catering cottage for four also available..

Mrs Stella Buckpitt, Middle Wastray Farm,
Blackawton, Totnes, Devon TQ9 7DD
Tel: 01803 712346
stella.buckpitt1@btopenworld.com
www.middle-wadstray-farm.com

Middle Wadstray

The South Devon Hotel with a Different Outlook...

Langstone Cliff Hotel

- Family Friendly • 66 En suite Bedrooms
- Indoor & Outdoor pools • Magnificent Sea Views
- Relaxation Therapies • Fitness Room • Hairdresser
- Tennis • Snooker • Table Tennis • Licensed Bars
- Extensive Lounges • 19 Acres of Grounds

Dawlish • South • Devon • EX7 0NA
Telephone 01626 868000
www.langstone-hotel.co.uk

AA
★★★
Hotel

symbols

	Totally non-smoking		Pets Welcome
	Children Welcome	SB	Short Breaks
	Suitable for Disabled Guests		Licensed

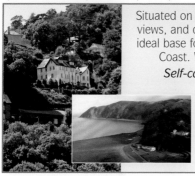

Situated on the South West Coastal Path with wonderful views, and delicious home cooking, the North Cliff is an ideal base for discovering Exmoor and the North Devon Coast. We welcome pets, children and groups.

Self-catering flat, sleeps 6, also available.

The North Cliff Hotel
North Walk, Lynton,
North Devon EX35 6HJ
Tel: 01598 752357
e-mail: holidays@northcliffhotel.co.uk
www.northcliffhotel.co.uk

SB

Great Sloncombe Farm
Moretonhampstead Devon TQ13 8QF
Tel: 01647 440595

Share the magic of Dartmoor all year round while staying in our lovely 13th century farmhouse full of interesting historical features. A working mixed farm set amongst peaceful meadows and woodland abundant in wild flowers and animals, including badgers, foxes, deer and buzzards. A welcoming and informal place to relax and explore the moors and Devon countryside. Comfortable double and twin rooms with en suite facilities, TV, central heating and coffee/tea making facilities. Delicious Devonshire breakfasts with new baked bread.

Open all year~No smoking~Farm Stay UK
e-mail: hmerchant@sloncombe.freeserve.co.uk • www.greatsloncombefarm.co.uk

AA
★★★★

Peace and Tranquillity are easily found at

A delightful 16th century Devon longhouse
in the beautiful Otter Valley

Fluxton Farm

Occupying a sheltered position just south of Ottery St Mary, and only 4 miles from the sea at Sidmouth. We are no longer a working farm, but keep ducks, chickens and geese, and have lots of cats.

We have 10 bedrooms, all en suite, and two charming sitting rooms. Our beamed dining room has a large open fire and separate tables, where a full English breakfast is served.

The house stands in peaceful, lawned gardens with a small trout stream flowing through.

As well as peace and quiet, we offer a warm welcome and an easy-going atmosphere, plus a high level of care and attention, comfort and delicious food.

• Children over 8 only.
• Pets welcome (not in public rooms)

Fluxton Farm, Ottery St Mary
Devon EX11 1RJ
Tel: 01404 812818 • Fax: 01404 814843 AA ★★
Proprietor Ann Forth • www.fluxtonfarm.co.uk

SB

Visit the FHG website
www.holidayguides.com
for details of the wide choice of accommodation
featured in the full range of FHG titles

Beera Farm

**Hilary Tucker
Beera Farm Milton Abbot,
Tavistock PL19 8PL
Tel & Fax: 01822 870216
Mobile: 07974 957966**

SB

Area of Outstanding Natural Beauty

- Delicious food served by trained chef. Special diets can be catered for.
- All rooms with en suite facilities (power shower), digital TV, hairdryer, toiletries etc.
- Children welcome - travel cot, bedding, highchair and children's meals can be provided.
- Lounge with cosy log fire in winter.
- Breakfast room with separate tables and views of garden and countryside.
- Free wireless broadband available.

**www.beera-farm.co.uk
hilary.tucker@farming.co.uk**

The Mill

A warm welcome awaits you at our converted mill, beautifully situated on the banks of the picturesque River Exe. Close to the National Trust's Knightshayes Court and on the route of the Exe Valley Way. Easy access to both the north and south coasts, Exmoor and Dartmoor. Only two miles from Tiverton. Relaxing and friendly atmosphere with delicious farmhouse fare. En suite bedrooms with TV and tea/coffee making facilities. *Bed and Breakfast from £26.*

SB

*Mrs L. Arnold, The Mill, Lower Washfield, Tiverton EX16 9PD • 01884 255297
e-mail: themillwashfield@hotmail.co.uk • www.themill-tiverton.co.uk*

Please note

All the information in this book is given in good faith in the belief that it is correct.

However, the publishers cannot guarantee the facts given in these pages, neither are

they responsible for changes in policy, ownership or terms that may take place after the

date of going to press. Readers should always satisfy themselves that the facilities they

require are available and that the terms, if quoted, still apply.

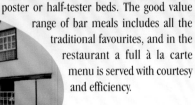

ORCHARD HOUSE

Horner, Halwell, Totnes, Devon TQ9 7LB • Telephone: 01548 821448
Helen@orchard-house-halwell.co.uk • www.orchard-house-halwell.co.uk

Tucked away in a rural valley of the South Hams,
only a short drive from sandy beaches and Dartmoor. With
mature gardens and private parking
surrounding the house, it is a peaceful location
from which to enjoy your stay.

Luxury accommodation in three spacious and beautifully furnished rooms, all en suite with colour TV, CD, radio, hair dryer, fridge and tea/coffee tray. Full central heating, sitting area has a log burner. Ample and varied breakfast using local produce. No smoking or pets.

From £27.50 to £30 pppn

BOUCHLAND FARM. *John and Eileen Chapple welcome you to spend a holiday on their family-run working farm, one mile off the A377 overlooking the lovely Taw Valley.*

Delicious home-cooking using fresh farm produce - full English breakfasts and varied four-course evening meal (optional). Family, double and twin rooms with washbasins, tea-making facilities and colour TV. En suite available. Lounge with TV, separate dining room, games room with snooker, darts and table tennis. **SB**

Ideal for exploring North Devon's sandy beaches, moors and many local places of interest.
Bed and Breakfast from £27.50 per person per night, reductions for children.

Bouchland Farm, Burrington, Umberleigh EX37 9NF • 01769 560394

symbols

 Totally non-smoking   Pets Welcome
 Children Welcome **SB** Short Breaks
 Suitable for Disabled Guests   Licensed

Dorset

Sandbanks, Dorset. Picture courtesy of Poole Tourism

SB

This charming old farmhouse was a monastery during the 16th century, restored in 1849 and is now a Listed building. A family-run working dairy farm, 140 acres overlooking the Blackmoor Vale. Accommodation is in three comfortable en suite rooms with colour TV and tea/coffee making facilities. Diningroom with inglenook fireplace, lounge with colour TV, for guests' use at all times. Also garden and lawn. Plenty of reading material and local information provided for this ideal touring area. Bed and Breakfast from £28. Excellent evening meals in all local inns nearby. Situated six miles from Sherborne with its beautiful Abbey and Castle.

SAE for further details. Mrs Jenny Mayo

Hermitage, Holnest, Sherborne, Dorset DT9 6HA
Tel and Fax: 01963 210296

Alms House Farm

A 15th century former Manor House that has retained some lovely historical features. Now a farmhouse on a family-run dairy and beef farm. It is in a beautiful rural location yet only five miles from the A303, two miles from A30 and two hours by train from London. An ideal place to relax and unwind, enjoy traditional home baking and a warm friendly atmosphere. Close to the abbey town of Sherborne, National Trust Properties and many other places of interest to suit all people.

Accommodation – one twin room en suite, one double room with a private bathroom, and lounge with colour TV and log fires.

Bed and Breakfast from £27pppn.
e-mail: stowellfarm@btconnect.com
www.stowellfarm.co.uk

AA
★★★★

Stowell Farm

Stowell, Near Sherborne DT9 4PE
Tel: 01963 370200 • Mrs E. Kingman

SB

Beech Farm

Sigwells, Charlton Horethorne, Near Sherborne, Dorset DT9 4LN • Mrs Susan Stretton

Comfortable farmhouse with relaxed atmosphere on our 137-acre farm, with beef and horses. A peaceful area on the Somerset/Dorset border with wonderful views from Corton Beacon.
Four miles from the old abbey town of Sherborne, six miles from Wincanton, and just two miles off the A303.
The farmhouse offers a double room en suite, a twin room, guest bathroom and an attic family room, all with TV and hospitality trays.

Bed and Breakfast £25 per person, less 10% for two or more nights.
Pets and horses by arrangement. • Open all year except Christmas.

Tel & Fax: 01963 220524
e-mail: beechfarm@sigwells.co.uk • www.sigwells.co.uk

Shillingstone, Sturminster Newton, Swanage

Pennhills Farmhouse, set in 100 acres of unspoiled countryside, is situated one mile from the village of Shillingstone in the heart of the Blackmore Vale, an ideal peaceful retreat, short break or holiday. It offers spacious comfortable accommodation for all ages; children welcome, pets by arrangement. One downstairs bedroom. All bedrooms en suite with TV and tea/coffee making facilities, complemented by traditional English breakfast with home produced bacon and sausages. Vegetarians catered for. Good meals available locally. Brochure sent on request. A warm and friendly welcome is assured from your host Rosie Watts. From £27 per person.

Mrs Rosie Watts, Pennhills Farm, Sandy Lane,
Off Lanchards Lane, Shillingstone, Blandford DT11 0TF
Tel: 01258 860491

Lower Fifehead Farm

Fifehead St Quinton, Sturminster Newton DT10 2AP
Tel: 01258 817335 (Lower Fifehead)
Tel: 01258 817896 (Honeysuckle House)

B&B £25-£35pppn

Come and have a relaxing holiday at Lower Fifehead Farm, staying in our lovely Listed farmhouse (pictured here), mentioned in Dorset books for its architectural interest, or in our new farmhouse called Honeysuckle House, actually on the farm, set within fields with outstanding views. We offer in both excellent breakfasts and tea/coffee making; Honeysuckle House also offers evening meals. Both farmhouses have guest lounges for you to relax in. We are within easy reach of the coast and all Dorset's beauty spots; excellent walking, riding and fishing can be arranged. Pets welcome in Honeysuckle; Lower Fifehead by arrangement. Lower Fifehead non-smoking; Honeysuckle non-smoking upstairs.
For Lower Fifehead Farm contact Mrs Jill Miller, for Honeysuckle House contact Mrs Jessica Miller

SB

A Victorian Purbeck stone farmhouse, on a working farm in the heart of the beautiful Isle of Purbeck. Family room en suite and one double with private shower room close by, both with colour TV and tea/coffee making facilities. Steam railway within walking distance, coastal path and sandy beaches three miles away. Excellent pubs and restaurants found locally. Open February 1st to November 30th. Bed and Breakfast from £25 per person.

Tel: 01929 480316
e-mail: downshayfarm@tiscali.co.uk
www.downshayfarm.co.uk

Downshay Farm

SB

Haycrafts Lane, Harmans Cross
Swanage, Dorset BH19 3EB

Looking for holiday accommodation?
for details of hundreds of properties
throughout the UK visit:

www.holidayguides.com

BANKES ARMS HOTEL

**East Street, Corfe Castle,
Wareham, Dorset BH20 5ED
Tel: 01929 480206
Fax: 01929 480186
bankescorfe@aol.com
www.dorset-hotel.co.uk**

In the shadow of historic Corfe Castle, this attractive, stone-built inn is ideally placed for a variety of holiday pleasures, being within easy reach of Swanage, Weymouth, Poole and Bournemouth.

Several real ales are on draught in company with light meals in the bar, and the à la carte restaurant specialises in fresh fish, game and traditional English fare.

There is a family room and a 200-seater beer garden with its own bar.

A delectable place in which to stay, providing comfortable and reasonably priced accommodation, all rooms having remote-control television and tea and coffee-making facilities.

SB

GLENTHORNE

CASTLE COVE, 15 OLD CASTLE ROAD, WEYMOUTH DT4 8QB

Secluded beachfront B&B in elegant Victorian villa and well equipped apartments with panoramic sea views of Olympic sailing area. Extensive gardens, heated pool, play areas, dog friendly beach, coastal path. Parking.

**Tel: 01305 777281 • Mobile: 07831 751526
e-mail: info@glenthorne-holidays.co.uk
www.glenthorne-holidays.co.uk
• Olivia Nurrish •**

Please note

All the information in this book is given in good faith in the belief that it is correct. However, the publishers cannot guarantee the facts given in these pages, neither are they responsible for changes in policy, ownership or terms that may take place after the date of going to press. Readers should always satisfy themselves that the facilities they require are available and that the terms, if quoted, still apply.

A useful index of towns/counties appears on pages 347-350

Gloucestershire

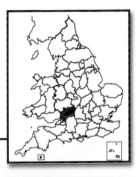

SB

A warm and friendly welcome awaits you at our completely refurbished 15th century Grade ll Listed farmhouse, in the heart of this beautiful village. Spacious beamed rooms, inglenook fireplace in dining room where a full English breakfast is served. Large private car park at rear. All bedrooms are en suite and have coffee/tea making facilities, TV, radio and hairdryer.

Accommodation comprises one double, two twin and one family suite consisting of a single and a double room en suite. Sorry no pets allowed in the house. Non-smoking. No children under 12.

Terms per night: from £65 per double-bedded suite, 2 persons sharing. More than two nights from £60. Family room for 3 persons sharing £85.

Veronica Stanley, Home Farm House, Ebrington, Chipping Campden GL55 6NL
Tel & Fax: 01386 593309 • e-mail: willstanley@farmersweekly.net
www.homefarminthecotswolds.co.uk

SB

Tel & Fax: 01452 840224

Quality all ground floor accommodation. "Kilmorie" is Grade II Listed (c1848) within conservation area in a lovely part of Gloucestershire. Double, twin, family or single bedrooms, all having tea tray, colour digital TV, radio, mostly en suite. Very comfortable guests' lounge, traditional home cooking is served in the separate diningroom overlooking large garden. Perhaps walk waymarked farmland footpaths which start here. Children may "help" with our pony, and "free range" hens. Rural yet perfectly situated to visit Cotswolds, Royal Forest of Dean, Wye Valley and Malvern Hills. Children over five years welcome. No smoking, please. Ample parking.

Bed and full English Breakfast from £24 per person

S.J. Barnfield, "Kilmorie Smallholding", Gloucester Road, Corse, Staunton, Gloucester GL19 3RQ
e-mail: sheila-barnfield@supanet.com; Mobile 07840 702218

SB

THE *Old*
Stocks Hotel
The Square,
Stow-on-the-Wold GL54 1AF

Ideal base for touring this beautiful area. Tasteful guest rooms in keeping with the hotel's old world character, yet with modern amenities. 3-terraced patio garden with smoking area.

AA

Mouth-watering menus offering a wide range of choices. Special bargain breaks also available.

Tel: 01451 830666 • Fax: 01451 870014
e-mail: fhg@oldstockshotel.co.uk
www.oldstockshotel.co.uk

Stow-on-the-Wold, Winchcombe

Somerset

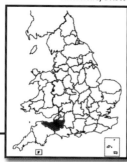

SB

THE YARN MARKET HOTEL
High Street, Dunster TA24 6SF

In the centre of quaint English village, an ideal location for walking and exploring Exmoor, the surrounding coastline and the many local attractions, The Yarn Market Hotel is a comfortable, family-run hotel which provides a friendly, relaxed atmosphere. All rooms are en suite, with tea and coffee making facilities, and colour TV. Some have four-poster beds, and some have views over the spectacular surrounding countryside. Family rooms are also available. The restaurant offers a mouth-watering selection of dishes featuring local produce whenever possible. Packed lunches available. Drying facilities. Non-smoking. Well-behaved pets are welcome. Party bookings and midweek breaks a speciality. B&B from £40.

Tel: 01643 821425   Fax: 01643 821475
e-mail: hotel@yarnmarkethotel.co.uk • www.yarnmarkethotel.co.uk

---

Bruneton House
Brompton Regis
Exmoor National Park
TA22 9NN

Built around 1625 for a wealthy landowner, Bruneton House offers spacious accommodation in three comfortable, south-facing bedrooms, each individually designed and equipped to the highest standards, with beverage facilities and a radio. There is a separate TV lounge overlooking a pretty cottage garden and the stunning Pulham Valley.

A full English breakfast is included in the nightly rate, and evening meals are available by arrangement, using fresh local produce whenever possible. Meal times are flexible and special diets can be catered for.

Brompton Regis nestles on the southern edge of Exmoor National Park, within easy reach of the north and south Devon coasts, where you will find beautiful beaches, fishing villages, and countless attractions for all the family. Set in some of the most beautiful countryside in the British Isles, Bruneton House is an ideal base for rambling, riding, twitching and fishing.

AA Red Star for Quality
(5 years running)
Tariff: from £26-£30pppn
Children under 12 half price.

For further information contact Mrs Jennifer Stringer Tel: 01398 371224 or e-mail: brunetonhouse@hotmail.com

SB

Modern farmhouse accommodation on a family-run working farm. Comfortable family home in beautiful gardens with views of Somerset Levels and Mendips. Quiet location, off the beaten track in lovely countryside. Breakfast room for sole use of guests. Full English breakfast. Meals available at local pub five minutes' walk away. En suite rooms with fridge, hairdryer, tea/coffee making facilities, shaver point, colour TV and central heating. Non-smoking.

Terms £28pppn, reduced rates for 3 nights or more.

Mrs Sheila Stott:
'LANA'
Hollow Farm,
Westbury-sub-Mendip,
Near Wells,
Somerset BA5 1HH
Tel: 01749 870635
sheila@stott2366.freeserve.co.uk

Malmesbury, Marlborough

Wiltshire

symbols

	Totally non-smoking		Pets Welcome
	Children Welcome	SB	Short Breaks
	Suitable for Disabled Guests		Licensed

London
(Central & Greater)

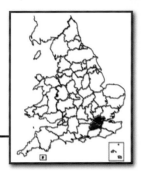

Elizabeth Hotel

Quiet, convenient townhouse overlooking the magnificent gardens of Eccleston Square. Only a short walk from Buckingham Palace and other tourist attractions. Easy access to Knightsbridge, Oxford Street and Regent Street. *Extremely reasonable rates in a fantastic location.*

Visa, Mastercard, Switch, Delta and JCB are all accepted.

37 Eccleston Square, Victoria, London SW1V 1PB

info@elizabethhotel.com
www.elizabethhotel.com
Tel: 020 7828 6812
Fax: 020 7828 6814

AA ★★★ Guest Accommodation

★★★ GUEST ACCOMMODATION

Visit the FHG website
www.holidayguides.com
for details of the wide choice of accommodation featured in the full range of FHG titles

Aylesbury

Buckinghamshire

This working family farm provides spacious, comfortable 4 Star Bed & Breakfast accommodation for couples and individuals, whether on an overnight visit or longer.
• Non-smoking • En suite bedrooms in 4 cottages with colour TV and tea/coffee tray
The Burnwode Jubilee Way cuts through the farm, and there are many places of historic interest in the area.

Ludgershall Road, Brill, Near Aylesbury, Bucks HP18 9TZ • Tel & Fax: 01844 238276
Bookings will only be taken by phone or fax
www.country-accom.co.uk/poletrees-farm

AA
★★★★

Poletrees Farm

Hampshire

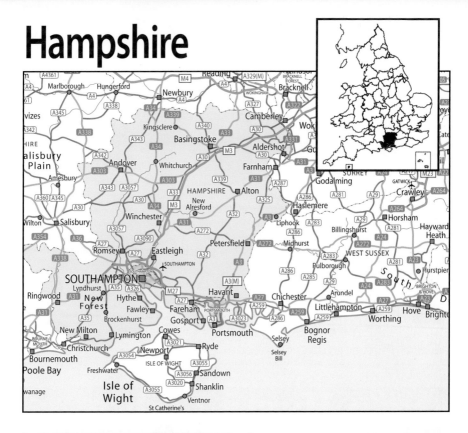

This late 17th century farmhouse, with its large garden, is open to guests throughout most of the year. Located quarter-of-a-mile west of the B2146 Petersfield to Chichester road, one-and-a-half-miles south of Petersfield, the house makes an ideal base for touring the scenic Hampshire and West Sussex countryside. Queen Elizabeth Country Park two miles adjoining picturesque village of Buriton at the western end of South Downs Way.

SB

Accommodation consists of 1 double (or family), 2 twin-bedded rooms all with private facilities; sittingroom & dining room. Full central heating. Children welcome, cot provided. Sorry, no pets. Car essential, ample parking adjoining the house. Non- smoking.

B&B £38pppn, reductions for children under 12 years.
Open all year except Christmas, March and April.

Mrs Mary Bray, Nursted Farm, Buriton, Petersfield GU31 5RW • 01730 264278

ℒang ℋouse
www.langhouse.co.uk

Winchester is one of the most beautiful cities in Britain and somewhere that demands exploration. Good accommodation is a must, and that is to be found at Lang House.

Built at the beginning of the 20th century it has all the graciousness of buildings of that time. You will be warm in winter and enjoy the cool airy rooms in summer. Ample parking in the grounds and the house overlooks the Royal Winchester Golf Course. All bedrooms have en suite facilities and are comfortable and well furnished with colour TV and tea/coffee making facilities. You can be assured of a warm and friendly welcome and Winchester has a plethora of good eateries.

Single from £50, double from £70.

**Lang House, 27 Chilbolton Avenue, Winchester SO22 5HE
Tel & Fax: 01962 860620**

Please note

All the information in this book is given in good faith in the belief that it is correct. However, the publishers cannot guarantee the facts given in these pages, neither are they responsible for changes in policy, ownership or terms that may take place after the date of going to press. Readers should always satisfy themselves that the facilities they require are available and that the terms, if quoted, still apply.

Totland

Isle of Wight

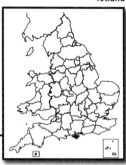

The Isle of Wight has several award-winning beaches, including Blue Flag winners, all of which are managed and maintained to the highest standard. Sandown, Shanklin and Ryde offer all the traditional delights; or head for Compton Bay where surfers brave the waves, fossil hunters admire the casts of dinosaur footprints at low tide, kitesurfers leap and soar across the sea and paragliders hurl themselves off the cliffs

Newport is the commercial centre of the Island with many famous high street stores and plenty of places to eat and drink. Ryde has a lovely Victorian Arcade lined with shops selling books and antiques. Cowes is great for sailing garb and Godshill is a treasure chest for the craft enthusiast. Lovers of fine food will enjoy the weekly farmers' markets selling home-grown produce and also the Garlic Festival held annually in August.

Many attractions are out of doors to take advantage of the Island's milder than average temperatures. However, if it should rain, there's plenty to choose from. There are vineyards offering wine tasting, cinemas, theatres and nightclubs as well as sports and leisure centres, a bowling alley and an ice skating rink, home to the Island's very own ice hockey team – the Wight Raiders.

The Island's diverse terrain makes it an ideal landscape for walkers and cyclists of all ages and abilities. Pony trekking and beach rides are also popular holiday pursuits and the Island's superb golf courses, beautiful scenery and temperate climate combine to make it the perfect choice for a golfing break.

Totland Bay

The Country Garden Hotel

A five minute stroll to the Solent, surrounded by lovely walks and hikes including Tennyson Downs and The Needles, and a short drive to the bustling port of Yarmouth. Set in lovely gardens, this quiet and intimate adults only hotel offers the best of all worlds for your holiday, including making your pet feel welcome! Excellent cuisine from our Chef of some thirteen years in our locally popular restaurant overlooking the gardens.

Garden, sea view and ground floor rooms available, all en suite with colour TV, fridge, duvets, down pillows, bathrobes, phone, central heating, hairdryer, tea & coffee and ample off-street parking.

Matthew and Beverley, resident proprietors, and a charming loyal staff of islanders are determined that every guest shall be delighted with the overall service, ambience, and special touches that make your stay a pleasantly memorable one.

ANY DAY TO ANY DAY,
B&B or HALF BOARD • ADULTS ONLY
Ferry inclusive rates October through April
For brochure, sample menu, tariff, and testimonials from recent guests, please

Phone/Fax: 01983 754 521
e-mail: countrygardeniow@aol.com • www.thecountrygardenhotel.co.uk
Church Hill, Totland Bay, Isle of Wight PO39 0ET

Kent

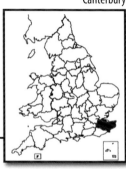

Canterbury, Deal, Dover

Bower Farmhouse Stelling Minnis Canterbury, Kent CT4 6BB

Tel: 01227 709430 • e-mail: nick@bowerbb.freeserve.co.uk • www.bowerfarmhouse.co.uk

Conveniently placed for historic Canterbury and the channel ports yet situated in total seclusion and quiet, the house is a charming heavily beamed 17th century Kentish Farm House. Sit down to breakfast, in front of the large inglenook, with fresh bread, garden laid eggs and fairtrade tea/coffee.

Enjoy delightful bedrooms, the gently sloping floor encouraging one bedwards after a delightful walk home across the common from one of the local hostelries. We have two doubles, both with en suite shower/ WC and a twin room with en suite bathroom.

Prices for 2009: Double/twin £65, or £48 for single occupancy.
Reductions for children. No charge for pets
A single room and self-catering accommodation are sometimes available.

Sutherland House Hotel

This stylish hotel offers comfortable accommodation in a pleasant residential area of the delightful seaside town of Deal, Kent. It's ideal for a quiet and peaceful stay in the atmosphere of an Edwardian House. Guests are encouraged to make themselves completely at home.

The five en suite bedrooms are decorated and furnished with great style and taste, with TV, tea/ coffee facilities and direct- dial telephone. The splendid dining room provides a charming venue for home-cooked dinners and breakfasts and guests have the use of a comfortable lounge well stocked with books and magazines. A fully stocked licensed bar is available for guests.

Sutherland House also benefits from a private car park. Sorry, no children under five years.

186 London Road, Deal CT14 9PT • Tel: 01304 362853 • Fax: 01304 381146

e-mail: info@sutherlandhouse.fsnet.co.uk • www.sutherlandhousehotel.co.uk

A useful index of towns/counties appears on pages 347-350

Manor Court Farm • Bed and Breakfast

Manor Court Farm Bed & Breakfast is offered in a spacious, listed Georgian farmhouse on a 350-acre family farm.

We aim to create a warm and friendly atmosphere so guests can relax and enjoy the farm and the surrounding lovely countryside of Kent and Sussex.

One double and two twin rooms are available throughout the year and are tastefully and comfortably furnished to a high standard. Each room has hot and cold water, tea making facilities, TV and wonderful views of the gardens and surrounding countryside. Our spacious bedrooms are complemented by two large bathroom/shower rooms, exclusively for guests use.

A lounge/sitting room with an open fire, television, and DVD and video players is available

Rates: from £28 per person per night.
Reduced rate for children. Babies free.

Mrs Julia Soyke, Manor Court Farm
Ashurst, Tunbridge Wells, Kent TN3 9TB
Telephone: 01892 740279
E-mail: jsoyke@jsoyke.freeserve.co.uk
www.manorcourtfarm.co.uk

Oxfordshire

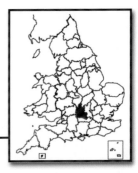

Please note

All the information in this book is given in good faith in the belief that it is correct.

However, the publishers cannot guarantee the facts given in these pages, neither are

they responsible for changes in policy, ownership or terms that may take place after the

date of going to press. Readers should always satisfy themselves that the facilities they

require are available and that the terms, if quoted, still apply.

Surrey

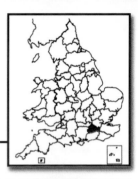

Stantons Hall Farm is an 18th century farmhouse, set in 18 acres of farmland and adjacent to Blindley Heath Common. Family, double and single rooms, most with WC, shower and wash-hand basins en suite. Separate bathroom. All rooms have colour TV, tea/coffee facilities and are centrally heated. Enjoy a traditional English breakfast in our large farmhouse kitchen.

Conveniently situated within easy reach of M25 (London Orbital), Gatwick Airport (car parking for travellers) and Lingfield Park racecourse.

• Bed and Breakfast from £30 per person, reductions for children sharing • Cot and high chair available
• Well behaved dogs welcome by prior arrangement • There are plenty of parking spaces.

Mrs V. Manwill, Stantons Hall Farm, Eastbourne Road, Blindley Heath, Lingfield RH7 6LG • 01342 832401

Sussex

East Sussex

West Sussex

Cambridgeshire

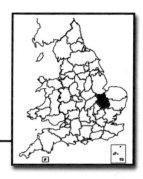

Essex

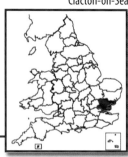

Essex - between London and England's East Coast lies the ancient county of Essex, a place of farms and forests, quiet villages and country towns, and also of seaside resorts offering traditional entertainments and exciting events. Thatched cottages and timber framed farmhouses are very characteristic as are the unmistakable outlines of windmills which still punctuate the horizon. Close to the European mainland, Essex has been influenced by many different cultures and historical events. The Normans left their mark in castles at Colchester, Castle Hedingham, Stansted and elsewhere, while Colchester's Roman walls remain to show the pedigree of Britain's oldest recorded town. Perhaps Essex is best known for its resorts. Southend, Clacton, Frinton, Walton and Dovercourt offer all the fun of the seaside but with much more besides. Down the centuries, Essex has been home to both the famous and the infamous. John Constable, England's greatest landscape painter, was inspired by the beauty of the Stour Valley; Hedingham Castle was once home to Edward de Vere, believed by many to be the true author of Shakespeare's works. Other famous names include the composers Gustav Holst and William Byrd, writers Dorothy L. Sayers, Sabine Baring-Gould and H.G. Wells, and the philosopher, John Locke.

Aylsham

Norfolk

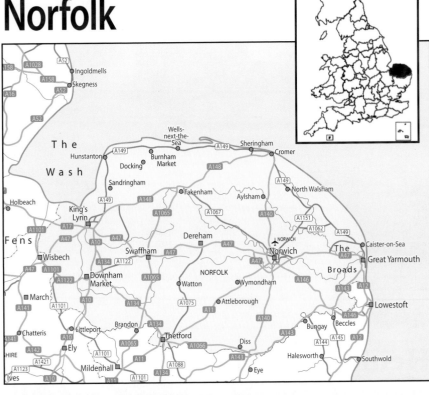

Publisher's note

While every effort is made to ensure accuracy, we regret that FHG Guides cannot accept responsibility for errors, misrepresentations or omissions in our entries or any consequences thereof. Prices in particular should be checked.

We will follow up complaints but cannot act as arbiters or agents for either party.

Heacham Manor

Opening Summer 2009

- 16th Century farmhouse developed into a luxury 4 star boutique hotel with 14 beautiful bedrooms with the finest of furniture and fittings
- Restaurant with a fabulous menu reflecting the wonderful local produce
- Beautiful gardens with arbours, ponds and secret sitting areas provide ideal surroundings to relax and unwind

- 18 hole championship length links style golf course and clubhouse
- Excellent location for North Norfolk's superb golf courses
- Luxury spa, thermal suite and swimming pool opening in 2010
- Beautiful countryside and coastal setting

Heacham Manor

Heacham Manor, Hunstanton Road, Heacham, Norfolk PE31 7JX T: **01485 536030**

www.heacham-manor.co.uk

Hempstead Hall

Holt, Norfolk NR25 6TN

SB

Enjoy a relaxing holiday with a friendly atmosphere in our 19th century flint farmhouse, beautifully set on a 300 acre arable farm with ducks, donkey and large gardens. Close to the north Norfolk coast and its many attractions. Take a ride on the steam train or a boat trip to Blakeney Point Seal Sanctuary. Large en suite family room, double with private bathroom. Colour TV, tea/coffee facilities. Large lounge with log burning stove. Children over 12 years only, please. Sorry, no pets indoors. B&B from £30-32 per person.

Tel: 01263 712224 • www.hempsteadhall.co.uk

Visit the FHG website

www.holidayguides.com

for details of the wide choice of accommodation

featured in the full range of FHG titles

ETC ★★★

HOLMDENE FARM

SB

BEESTON, KING'S LYNN PE32 2NJ

17th century farmhouse situated in central Norfolk within easy reach of the coast and Broads. Sporting activities available locally, village pub nearby. One double room, one twin and two singles. Pets welcome. Bed and Breakfast from £22.50 per person; Evening Meal from £15. Weekly terms available and child reductions. Two self-catering cottages. Sleeping 4/8. Terms on request.

**MRS G. DAVIDSON • Tel: 01328 701284
e-mail: holmdenefarm@farmersweekly.net
www.holmedenefarm.co.uk**

Greenacres Farmhouse

Woodgreen, Long Stratton, Norwich NR15 2RR
Period 17th century farmhouse on 30 acre common with ponds and natural wildlife, 10 miles south of Norwich (A140). The beamed sittingroom with inglenook fireplace invites you to relax. A large sunny dining room encourages you to enjoy a leisurely traditional breakfast. All en suite bedrooms (two double/twin) are tastefully furnished to complement the oak beams and period furniture, with tea/coffee facilities and TV. Full size snooker table and all-weather tennis court for guests' use. Jo is trained in therapeutic massage, aromatherapy and reflexology and is able to offer this to guests who feel it would be of benefit. Come and enjoy the peace and tranquillity of our home. *Bed and Breakfast from £30. Reductions for two nights or more. Non-smoking.*

Tel: 01508 530261 • www.abreakwithtradition.co.uk

Please note

All the information in this book is given in good faith in the belief that it is correct.

However, the publishers cannot guarantee the facts given in these pages, neither are they responsible for changes in policy, ownership or terms that may take place after the date of going to press. Readers should always satisfy themselves that the facilities they require are available and that the terms, if quoted, still apply.

WHINCLIFF
Bed & Breakfast
CROMER ROAD
MUNDESLEY
NR11 8DU
Tel: 01263 721554

A warm welcome to all pets and their owners at "Whincliff" by the sea. Family/en suite, twin or single room available. Tea/coffee facilities, TV in all rooms, private parking, sea views, unspoilt beach and coastal walks to enjoy.

Anne & Alan Cutler
e-mail: cutler.a@sky.com

Home Farm

Comfortable accommodation set in four acres, quiet location, secluded garden. Conveniently situated off A11 between Attleborough and Wymondham, an excellent location for Snetterton and only 20 minutes from Norwich and 45 minutes from the Norfolk Broads. Accommodation comprises two double rooms and one single-bedded room, all with TV, tea/coffee facilities and central heating. Children over five years old welcome, but sorry no animals and no smoking. Fishing lakes only ½ mile away.

Bed and Breakfast from £27 pppn.

Mrs Joy Morter, Home Farm,
Morley, Wymondham NR18 9SU
Tel: 01953 602581

Suffolk

Derbyshire

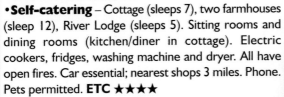

Herefordshire

Herefordshire lies on the border with Wales, but is merely a stone's throw from Birmingham, Bristol, the Cotswolds and Cardiff. Green countryside, meandering rivers and acres of traditional cider orchards make up the landscape of this most rural of counties. It is home to the Hereford breed of cattle and has since become recognised for the standard of its local food and drink. Hereford is a Cathedral City but with the feel of a market town offering visitors an interesting array of shops, cafes and bistros. The Norman Cathedral is home to the world famous Mappa Mundi, the oldest map of the world, and to the largest Chained Library in the world. The five market towns (Bromyard, Kington, Ledbury, Leominster and Ross-on-Wye) all offer something different to delight the visitor, and the 'Black and White Village' Trail explores a group of villages with beautiful half-timbered houses, cottages and country inns.

Moor Court Farm
Bed and Breakfast

Discover this beautiful 15th century timber-framed farmhouse with its spacious gardens. Set in its own 500 acres, we are easy to find, yet ideally located for access to the local towns of Hereford, Ledbury, Leominster, Bromyard, Ross-on-Wye, Ludlow and Malvern, with the Wye Valley, Black Mountains, Brecon Beacons and the Malvern Hills only a short drive away.

Guests will enjoy spacious en suite bedrooms including a four-poster room, all of which are beautifully furnished. Separate dining room and guests' lounge - ideal for family groups to unwind together at the end of an eventful day. Centrally heated throughout to ensure a comfortable stay. Fabulous catering using fine local ingredients and a variety of local wines. Healthy and wholesome breakfast.

Open all year. Terms from £25 per person based on two sharing, £27 single. Evening meal from £15.
Self-catering holiday cottage also available (sleeps 5).

Moor Court Farm B&B, Stretton Grandison, Ledbury HR8 2TP
Tel: 01531 670408 • www.moorcourtfarm.co.uk

Thatch Close, Llangrove, Ross-on-Wye HR9 6EL

Secluded, peaceful, comfortable Georgian farmhouse, yet convenient for A40, M4 and M50. Our three lovely bedrooms, all en suite, have magnificent views over the unspoilt countryside. Relax in the visitors' lounge or sit in the shade of mature trees in our garden. You may be greeted by our dog or free flying parrot. Terms from £35 per person (sharing). Please telephone or e-mail for brochure.
Wildlife Action Gold Award.

Mrs M.E. Drzymalski (01989 770300)

AA ★★★★ Guest Accommodation

e-mail: info@thatchclose.co.uk • website: www.thatchclose.co.uk

symbols

⊘	**Totally non-smoking**			**Pets Welcome**
	Children Welcome		**SB**	**Short Breaks**
♿	**Suitable for Disabled Guests**		♟	**Licensed**

Leicestershire & Rutland

Alford

Lincolnshire

Please note

All the information in this book is given in good faith in the belief that it is correct.
However, the publishers cannot guarantee the facts given in these pages, neither are
they responsible for changes in policy, ownership or terms that may take place after the
date of going to press. Readers should always satisfy themselves that the facilities they
require are available and that the terms, if quoted, still apply.

Market Rasen

Please note

A useful index of towns/counties appears on pages 347-350

Please note

All the information in this book is given in good faith in the belief that it is correct.

However, the publishers cannot guarantee the facts given in these pages, neither are they responsible for changes in policy, ownership or terms that may take place after the date of going to press. Readers should always satisfy themselves that the facilities they require are available and that the terms, if quoted, still apply.

Stixwould Road,
Woodhall Spa LN10 6QG
Tel: 01526 352411
Fax: 01526 353473
reception@petwood.co.uk
www.petwood.co.uk

Originally built in the early 1900s The Petwood Hotel stands in 30 acres of mature woodland and gardens. During World War II, 617 Squadron, known as the "Dambusters", used the hotel as their Officers' Mess. Today it is a country house hotel of unique charm, offering a high standard of comfort and hospitality in elegant surroundings. All bedrooms are fully equipped to meet the needs of today's discerning guests, and the highly recommended Tennysons Restaurant offers the very best of English and Continental cuisine. There are ample leisure opportunities available locally as well as tranquil villages and historic market towns to explore.

AA ★★★

★★★ HOTEL

Northamptonshire

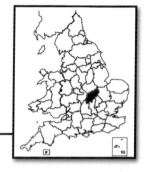

ENJOY A HOLIDAY in our comfortable 17th century farmhouse with oak beams and inglenook fireplaces. Four-poster bed now available. Peaceful surroundings, large garden containing ancient circular dovecote. Dairy Farm is a working farm situated in a beautiful Northamptonshire village just off the A14, within easy reach of many places of interest or ideal for a restful holiday. Good farmhouse food and friendly atmosphere. Open all year, except Christmas. Bed and Breakfast from £28 to £40; (children under 10 half price); Evening Meal £17.

Mrs A. Clarke, Dairy Farm, Cranford St Andrew, Kettering NN14 4AQ
Telephone: 01536 330273

Nottinghamshire

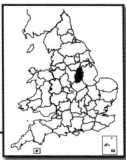

Shropshire

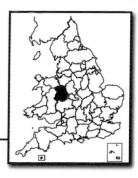

Shropshire is perhaps less well-known than other English counties. This is despite being the birthplace of Charles Darwin, home to the world's first iron bridge (now a World Heritage Site), having not one, but two of the finest medieval towns in England, inspiring the creation of the modern Olympics, and being the kingdom of the real King Arthur. After all, Shropshire is easy enough to find and get to from almost anywhere. (Hint: just north of Birmingham or south of Manchester depending on your direction of travel, and sitting snugly on the Welsh borders). It may also come as a surprise to find out just how much is on offer. There are plenty of indoor and outdoor attractions, so the weather isn't a problem either. In Ironbridge, you can step into the past at the Ironbridge Gorge Museums where you'll find 10 museums to visit, all following the history of the Industrial Revolution. For retail therapy at its best, small independent shops can be found in all its market towns, full of those special 'somethings' you were looking for and even some things you weren't.

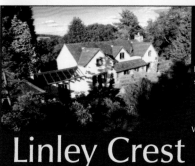

Court Farm

Court Farm is a listed farmhouse, sympathetically renovated to provide guests with four-star rated en suite accommodation. One twin and one double room are available with views over the farmhouse garden and are positioned away from the owner's quarters for added privacy and peacefulness. Set on a working farm, the surrounding countryside is ideal for walking and we are perfectly located to explore Ironbridge, Shrewsbury, Bridgnorth and Much Wenlock, and the wealth of eateries in and around Ludlow. There is also an abundance of National Trust properties, beautiful gardens and English Heritage sites to choose from.

Mrs Alison Norris, Court Farm, Gretton,Church Stretton SY6 7HU
Tel: 01694 771219
www.courtfarm.eu

AA ★★★★ Guest Accommodation

Olde worlde beamed farmhouse situated amidst spectacular scenery at the lower slopes of the Long Mynd Hills. We are a working farm producing beef cattle and sheep. One double bedroom and one twin, both with en suite bathroom, colour TV, hairdryer and tea tray. Good farmhouse cooking is served in the dining room. Private guests' sitting room.

AA ★★★ Farmhouse

Malt House Farm

Non-smoking • Regret no children or pets

Bed and Breakfast from £25pppn • Evening meal from £15 per person

Malt House Farm, Lower Wood, Church Stretton SY6 6LF
Tel: 01694 751379 • Proprietor: Mrs Lyn Bloor

SB

Lovely 17th century farmhouse in peaceful village amidst the beautiful South Shropshire Hills, an Area of Outstanding Natural Beauty. The farmhouse is full of character and all rooms have heating and are comfortable and spacious. The bedrooms are either en suite or private bathroom with hairdryers, tea/coffee making facilities, patchwork quilts and colour TV. There is a lounge with colour TV and inglenook fireplace. Children welcome. We are a working farm, centrally situated for visiting Ironbridge, Shrewsbury and Ludlow, each being easily reached within half an hour. Touring and walking information is available for visitors. Bed and full English Breakfast from £26pppn. Non-smoking. Open all year excluding November, December and January.

Mrs Mary Jones, Acton Scott Farm, Acton Scott, Church Stretton SY6 6QN • Tel: 01694 781260
Fax: 0870-129 4591 • e-mail: fhg@actonscottfarm.co.uk • www.actonscottfarm.co.uk

★★★ GUEST ACCOMMODATION

Froghall (near Cheadle), Kingsley

Staffordshire

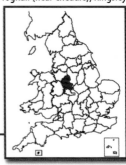

Warwickshire

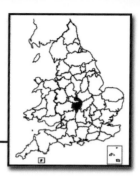

Monks Barn Farm

Shipston Road,
Stratford-upon-Avon,
Warwickshire CV37 8NA
Tel: 01789 293714

Monks Barn Farm is situated 2 miles south of Stratford on the A3400. Dating back to the 16th century, the farm lies along the banks of the River Stour. Now modernised, it still preserves the old character, and offers first-class amenities; some accommodation is separate from the main house. Ground floor rooms available. Pleasant riverside walks to the village of Clifford Chambers. Centrally situated for visiting Stratford, Warwick and the Cotswolds. Three double, two twin, one family and one single room, most en suite. Children of all ages welcome. Non-smoking.

B&B from £26-£28.50. Credit cards accepted.

ritameadows@btconnect.com • www.monksbarnfarm.com

Visit the FHG website
www.holidayguides.com
for details of the wide choice of accommodation
featured in the full range of FHG titles

West Midlands

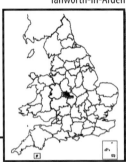

symbols

Totally non-smoking			Pets Welcome

- Totally non-smoking
- Children Welcome
- Suitable for Disabled Guests
- Pets Welcome
- **SB** Short Breaks
- Licensed

Worcester

Croft Guest House
Bransford, Worcester
WR6 5JD

B&B from £28 to £38 single £47 to £65 double

16th-18th century part black-and-white cottage-style country house situated in the Teme Valley, four miles from Worcester and Malvern. Croft House is central for visiting numerous attractions in Worcester, Hereford, the Severn Valley and surrounding countryside. River and lake fishing are close by, and an 18-hole golf course opposite. Comfortable, non-smoking house. Three en suite guest rooms (two double, one family) and one with washbasin are available. Rooms are double glazed and have colour TV, radio alarm, hairdryer and courtesy tray. TV lounge, residential licence. Dogs welcome by arrangement.

Full English breakfast is prepared from home-grown/made produce in season.

Ann & Brian Porter • Tel: 01886 832227
e-mail: hols@brianporter.orangehome.co.uk • www.croftguesthouse.com

A useful index of towns/counties appears on pages 347-350

FHG Guides
publish a large range of well-known accommodation guides.
We will be happy to send you details or you can use the order form
at the back of this book.

MOSELEY FARM
BED AND BREAKFAST
Moseley Road, Hallow,
Worcester WR2 6NL
Tel: 01905 641343
Fax: 01905 641416

Spacious 17th Century former
farmhouse with countryside views.
Rural location four miles from
Worcester. Providing comfortable
accommodation.

SB

Room only during the week from £25 per night;
full English breakfast at weekends.
Two en suite family rooms and two standard rooms.
Colour TV, radio alarm clocks,
tea/coffee making facilities and free wifi.

e-mail: moseleyfarmbandb@aol.com
www.moseleyfarmbandb.co.uk

Ratings & Awards

For the first time ever the AA, VisitBritain, VisitScotland, and the Wales Tourist Board will use a single method of assessing and rating serviced accommodation. Irrespective of which organisation inspects an establishment the rating awarded will be the same, using a common set of standards, giving a clear guide of what to expect. The RAC is no longer operating an Hotel inspection and accreditation business.

Accommodation Standards: Star Grading Scheme

Using a scale of 1-5 stars the objective quality ratings give a clear indication of accommodation standard, cleanliness, ambience, hospitality, service and food, This shows the full range of standards suitable for every budget and preference, and allows visitors to distinguish between the quality of accommodation and facilities on offer in different establishments. All types of board and self-catering accommodation are covered, including hotels,
B&Bs, holiday parks, campus accommodation, hostels, caravans and camping, and boats.

VisitBritain and the regional tourist boards, enjoyEngland.com, VisitScotland and VisitWales, and the AA have full details of the grading system on their websites

The more stars, the higher level of quality

★★★★★
exceptional quality, with a degree of luxury

★★★★
excellent standard throughout

★★★
very good level of quality and comfort

★★
good quality, well presented and well run

★
acceptable quality; simple, practical, no frills

National Accessible Scheme

If you have particular mobility, visual or hearing needs, look out for the National Accessible Scheme. You can be confident of finding accommodation or attractions that meet your needs by looking for the following symbols.

 Typically suitable for a person with sufficient mobility to climb a flight of steps but would benefit from fixtures and fittings to aid balance

 Typically suitable for a person with restricted walking ability and for those that may need to use a wheelchair some of the time and can negotiate a maximum of three steps

 Typically suitable for a person who depends on the use of a wheelchair and transfers unaided to and from the wheelchair in a seated position. This person may be an independent traveller

 Typically suitable for a person who depends on the use of a wheelchair in a seated position. This person also requires personal or mechanical assistance (eg carer, hoist).

Yorkshire

North Yorkshire

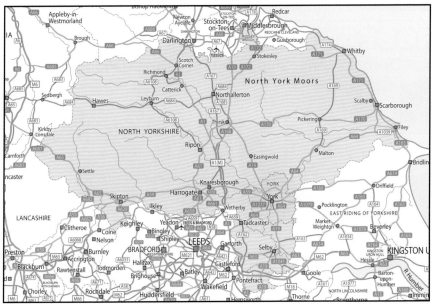

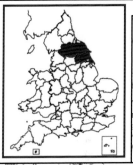

East Yorkshire

South
& West Yorkshire

East Yorkshire

A useful index of towns/counties appears on pages 347-350

North Yorkshire

MILTON HOUSE

Askrigg is situated in the heart of Wensleydale and is within easy reach of many interesting places – Aysgarth Falls, Hardraw Falls, Bolton Castle. Askrigg is one of the loveliest villages in the dale. This is an ideal area for touring or walking. Milton House is a lovely spacious house with all the comforts of home, beautifully furnished and decor to match. All bedrooms are en suite with colour TV and tea/coffee making facilities. Visitors' lounge, dining room. Central heating. Private parking. Milton House is open all year for Bed and Breakfast.
Good pub food nearby. You are sure of a friendly welcome and a homely atmosphere. Please write or phone Mrs Beryl Percival for details and brochure.

Askrigg, Leyburn DL8 3HJ • Tel: 01969 650217
e-mail: stay-miltonhouse@btinternet.com • www.miltonhousebandb.co.uk

---

SB

Peacefully situated farmhouse away from the madding crowd.

B&B with optional Evening Meal • Home cooking.

Pets sleep where you prefer.

Ideally positioned for exploring the beautiful Yorkshire Dales.

**Mrs Julie Clarke, Middle Farm,
Woodale, Coverdale, Leyburn,
North Yorkshire DL8 4TY 01969 640271
e-mail: j-a-clarke@hotmail.co.uk**

www.yorkshirenet.co.uk/stayat/middlefarm/index.htm

ROWANTREE FARM is a family-run dairy farm situated in the heart of the North York Moors. Ideal walking and mountain biking area, with panoramic moorland views. Coast easily accessible. Our non-smoking home comprises one family room and one twin-bedded room, with private bathroom and private shower room, also full central heating, beverage tray, CD clock radio and hairdryer. Relax in our residents' lounge with colour TV/video. Ample car parking.

Rowantree Farm

* *Children welcome; cot and high chair available.*
* *Good home cooking (vegetarians catered for), served in our separate dining room. Packed lunches available.*
* *B&B from £25; Evening Meal by prior arrangement.*

Mrs L. Tindall, Rowantree Farm, Ainthorpe, Whitby YO21 2LE • 01287 660396
e-mail: krbsatindall@aol.com • www.rowantreefarm.co.uk

Readers are requested to mention this FHG
guidebook when seeking accommodation

Glaisdale, Harrogate

Red House Farm

Listed Georgian farmhouse featured in "Houses of the North York Moors". Completely refurbished to the highest standards, retaining all original features. Bedrooms have bath/shower/toilet, central heating, TV and tea making facilities. Excellent walks straight from the doorstep. Friendly farm animals – a few cows, horses, geese and pretty free-roaming hens. One-and-a-half acres of gardens, sitting-out areas. Magnificent views. Interesting buildings – Listed barns now converted to 3 holiday cottages. Games room with snooker table. Eight miles from seaside/Whitby. Village pub within walking distance. Stabling available for horses/dogs. Non-smoking.

SB

Tom and Sandra Spashett, Red House Farm, Glaisdale,
Near Whitby YO21 2PZ • Tel & Fax: 01947 897242
e-mail: spashettredhouse@aol.com
www.redhousefarm.com

Homely, comfortable, Christian accommodation. Spacious stone built bungalow in beautiful Nidderdale which is very central for touring the Yorkshire Dales; Pateley Bridge two miles, Harrogate 14 miles, Ripon nine miles. Museums, rocks,

SB

caves, fishing, bird watching, beautiful quiet walks, etc all nearby. En suite rooms (one twin, two double), TV. Private lounge. Tea making facilities available. Choice of breakfast. Evening meals available one mile away. Ample parking space on this working farm. Open Easter to end of October.

Mrs C.E. Nelson, Nidderdale Lodge Farm,
Fellbeck, Pateley Bridge, Harrogate HG3 5DR
Tel: 01423 711677

Banavie

is a large semi-detached house set in a quiet part of the picturesque village of Thornton-le-Dale, one of the prettiest villages in Yorkshire with its famous thatched cottage and bubbling stream flowing through the centre. We offer our guests a quiet night's sleep and rest away from the main road, yet only four minutes' walk from the village centre. One large double or twin bedroom and two double bedrooms, all tastefully decorated with en suite facilities, colour TV, hairdryer, shaver point etc. and tea/coffee making facilities. There is a large guest lounge, tea tray on arrival. A real Yorkshire breakfast is served in the dining room. Places to visit include Castle Howard, Eden Camp, North Yorkshire Moors Railway, Goathland ("Heartbeat"), York etc. There are three pubs, a bistro and a fish and chip shop for meals. Children and dogs welcome. Own keys. Car parking at back of house.

B&B from £27pppn
• SAE please for brochure • Welcome to Excellence
• Hygiene Certificate held • No Smoking
Mrs Ella Bowes

BANAVIE, ROXBY ROAD, THORNTON-LE-DALE, PICKERING YO18 7SX
Tel: 01751 474616 • e-mail: info@banavie.uk.com • www.banavie.uk.com

---

One twin and one double en suite rooms, one single; all with tea/coffee making facilities and TV; alarm clock/radio and hairdryer also provided; diningroom; central heating.

ETC ★★★★

Very clean and comfortable accommodation with good food. Situated in a quiet part of this picturesque village, which is in a good position for Moors, "Heartbeat" country, coast, North

Tangalwood
Roxby Road, Thornton-le-Dale, Pickering YO18 7TQ

York Moors Railway, Flamingo Park Zoo and forest drives, mountain biking and walking. Good facilities for meals provided in the village. Open Easter to October for Bed and Breakfast from £28-£32pp. Private car park. Secure motorbike and cycle storage.

TELEPHONE: **01751 474688** • **www.accommodation.uk.net/tangalwood**

Browson Bank Farmhouse Accommodation

A newly converted granary set in 300 acres of farmland. The accommodation consists of three very tastefully furnished double/twin rooms all en suite, tea and coffee making facilities, colour TV and central heating. A large, comfortable lounge is available to relax in. Full English breakfast served. Situated six miles West of Scotch Corner (A1). Ideal location to explore the scenic countryside of Teesdale and the Yorkshire Dales and close to the scenic towns of Barnard Castle and Richmond. Terms from £25 per night.

**Browson Bank Farmhouse, Browson Bank, Dalton, Richmond DL11 7HE
Tel: (01325) 718504 • Mobile: 07703 325088 • www.browsonbank.co.nr**

HOGARTH HALL
Boggle Hole Road, Near Robin Hood's Bay, Whitby YO22 4QQ
Tel: 01947 880547

Hogarth Hall is set in 145 acres of habitat attracting a variety of wildlife, wonderful views over ancient woodlands, heather-covered moorland and down the valley to the sea. Enjoy wonderful sunsets and sunrises.

All rooms are en suite. TV; tea/coffee making facilities are available.

Scarborough 12 miles • Whitby 9 miles • York 40 miles • Rievaulx Abbey 30 miles.

Walks around the farm and further afield. Robin Hood's Bay is a 1 hr 20 min. walk along the road, unused railway, cliff path or beach. Use your car to visit points of interest listed on our tour.

Details from David and Angela Pattinson.

SCARBOROUGH Sue and Tony Hewitt, Harmony Country Lodge, Limestone Road, Burniston, Scarborough YO13 0DG (0800 2985840; Tel & Fax: 01723 870276). DISTINCTIVELY DIFFERENT. Peaceful and relaxing retreat, octagonal in design and set in two acres of private grounds with 360° panoramic views of the National Park and sea. An ideal centre for walking or touring. Two miles from Scarborough and within easy reach of Whitby, York and the beautiful North Yorkshire countryside. Tastefully decorated en suite centrally heated rooms with colour TV and all with superb views. Attractive dining room, guest lounge and relaxing conservatory. Traditional English breakfast, including vegetarian. Licensed. Private parking facilities. Personal service and warm, friendly Yorkshire hospitality.

SB

Rates: Bed and Breakfast from £29 to £37.
• Non-smoking. • Children over 7 years welcome. • Spacious 5-berth caravan also available for self-catering holidays.
ETC ★★★★
e-mail: mail@harmonylodge.net   www.harmonycountrylodge.co.uk

THIRSK Mrs M. Fountain, Town Pasture Farm, Boltby, Thirsk YO7 2DY (01845 537298).
A warm welcome awaits on a 180 acre mixed farm in beautiful Boltby village, nestling in the valley below the Hambleton Hills, in the midst of Herriot country and on the edge of the North York Moors National Park. An 18th century stone-built farmhouse with full central heating, comfortable en suite bedrooms (one family, one twin) with original old oak beams, and tea/coffee facilities; spacious guests' lounge with colour TV. Good home cooking, hearty English breakfast. Ideal walking country and central for touring the Dales, York and East Coast. Pony trekking in village.
• Working farm. • Children welcome. • Pets welcome.
Rates: Bed and Breakfast from £28 - £35
ETC ★★★★

Receive a warm welcome at this family-run guesthouse. Enjoy breakfast in our attractive conservatory or outside on our beautiful patio. York House is approximately 10 minutes' walk from York Minster and is the perfect base for a visit to York or the surrounding areas. Rooms offer all the conveniences you could need for a relaxing and enjoyable stay.

Some of the facilities offered:
en suite shower or bath facilities • four-poster • double, twin, family and single rooms • tea/coffee making facilities • off-street parking • full English/vegetarian breakfast. • *No smoking establishment* • *Prices from £29pppn.* • *Free wifi access* • *Children welcome*

York House
62 Heworth Green,
York YO31 7TQ

Tel & Fax: 01904 427070 • David and Katherine Leedham
e-mail: yorkhouse.bandb@tiscali.co.uk
www.yorkhouseyork.com

Please note

All the information in this book is given in good faith in the belief that it is correct. However, the publishers cannot guarantee the facts given in these pages, neither are they responsible for changes in policy, ownership or terms that may take place after the date of going to press. Readers should always satisfy themselves that the facilities they require are available and that the terms, if quoted, still apply.

Durham

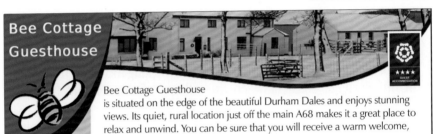

Bee Cottage Guesthouse

Bee Cottage Guesthouse is situated on the edge of the beautiful Durham Dales and enjoys stunning views. Its quiet, rural location just off the main A68 makes it a great place to relax and unwind. You can be sure that you will receive a warm welcome,

All eight bedrooms have en-suite shower rooms, TV, tea-making facilities and hairdryer. Some ground floor rooms are available. There are two conservatory dining rooms and two guests' lounges, all of which have lovely views. Ample car parking.

Home cooked food with a choice of dinner menu. Vegetarians catered for. Licensed to sell alcohol.

Bee Cottage makes a great base for walking and cycling. It is within easy reach of Durham, Newcastle, Beamish Museum, Hadrian's Wall, Barnard Castle, Weardale, Northumberland coast and much more.

Irene Mordey and David Blackburn
BEE COTTAGE FARMHOUSE, CASTLESIDE, CONSETT DH8 9HW
Tel: 01207 508224
e-mail: beecottage68@aol.com • www.beecottage.co.uk

Visit the FHG website
www.holidayguides.com
for details of the wide choice of accommodation
featured in the full range of FHG titles

Northumberland

Alndyke Farmhouse B&B

Alndyke Farmhouse is a Georgian Grade II Listed farmhouse set in 500 acres of arable farmland which has been in the Davison family for 3 generations.

All the en suite guest rooms are spacious and tastefully decorated, with colour TV, radio alarm and hairdryer. A hospitality tray is provided on arrival, with tea, coffee and home-made shortbread. Breakfast is served in the south-facing dining room which enjoys great countryside views. The relaxing guest lounge has a wood burning stove - sit back with a good book, enjoy the view or watch TV.

Alndyke is perfect for visiting Northumberland - 10 minutes by car to the beach, and a 30 minute walk to the historic town of Alnwick with its castle and gardens.

Strictly non-smoking. Private car park.

Alnmouth Road, Alnwick NE66 3PB

Tel: 01665 510252 • e-mail: laura@alndyke.co.uk • www.alndyke.co.uk

---

Situated one minute from Berwick-upon-Tweed's main thoroughfare this hotel is surrounded by walls and ramparts built by Queen Elizabeth I to protect Berwick. Accommodation consists of two family rooms, one double, one twin/triple and one single room (can sleep up to 14). All are en suite with colour TV, tea/coffee, central heating, hairdryer, trouser press and ironing facilities. A wide range of attractions and activities are on offer with lots of beaches and picnic areas within easy walking distance. Ideal centre point for visits to Edinburgh and Newcastle. Private parking. Restaurant and bar lounge. Vegetarians also catered for.

Fred and Lynda Miller, Cobbled Yard Hotel,
40 Walkergate, Berwick-upon-Tweed, Northumberland TD15 1DJ

Tel: 01289 308 407 • Fax: 01289 330 623
e-mail: allmail@cobbledyardhotel.onyxnet.co.uk
www.cobbledyardhotel.com

The Cobbled Yard Hotel

Friendly Hound Cottage
Ford Common,
Berwick-upon-Tweed TD15 2QD

Set in a quiet rural location, convenient for Holy Island, Berwick, Bamburgh and the Heritage coastline. Come and enjoy our top quality accommodation, excellent breakfasts, and warm welcome. *Arrive as our guests and leave as our friends.*

Tel: 01289 388554 • www.friendlyhoundcottage.co.uk

Visit the FHG website

www.holidayguides.com

for details of the wide choice of accommodation

featured in the full range of FHG titles

Katerina's Guest House

High Street, Rothbury NE65 7TQ • 01669 620691   SB

Charming old guest house, ideally situated for the amenities of pretty Rothbury village, and to explore Northumberland's hills, coast, Alnwick Castle and gardens. Beautiful bedrooms, each decorated and colour co-ordinated to enhance its individual character; some with original stone fireplaces/beamed ceilings, all en suite, with four-poster beds, TV, and superbly stocked tea tray (with home-made scones!). Wide, interesting choice of breakfasts; licensed evening meals also available – sample Cath's bread, 'whisky porridge', vegetarian nutballs, or Steak Katerina.

Bed and Breakfast from £64-£74 per room per night, depending on number of nights booked.

e-mail: cath@katerinasguesthouse.co.uk
www.katerinasguesthouse.co.uk

Please note

All the information in this book is given in good faith in the belief that it is correct. However, the publishers cannot guarantee the facts given in these pages, neither are they responsible for changes in policy, ownership or terms that may take place after the date of going to press. Readers should always satisfy themselves that the facilities they require are available and that the terms, if quoted, still apply.

Other specialised holiday guides from FHG

PUBS & INNS OF BRITAIN • **COUNTRY HOTELS** OF BRITAIN

WEEKEND & SHORT BREAK HOLIDAYS IN BRITAIN

THE GOLF GUIDE WHERE TO PLAY, WHERE TO STAY

500 GREAT PLACES TO STAY • **SELF-CATERING HOLIDAYS** IN BRITAIN

BED & BREAKFAST STOPS • **CARAVAN & CAMPING HOLIDAYS**

FAMILY BREAKS IN BRITAIN

Published annually: available in all good bookshops or direct from the publisher:
FHG Guides, Abbey Mill Business Centre, Seedhill, Paisley PA1 1TJ
Tel: 0141 887 0428 • Fax: 0141 889 7204
e-mail: admin@fhguides.co.uk • www.holidayguides.com

Tyne & Wear

New Kent Hotel

**127 Osborne Road,
Jesmond,
Newcastle-upon-Tyne
NE2 2TB**
Tel: 0191-281 7711
Fax: 0191-281 3369

This privately owned hotel is situated in a quiet location, but only minutes from the city centre. It has built up a reputation for good food and friendly, efficient service in a warm and congenial atmosphere. All bedrooms are en suite, with hospitality tray, direct-dial telephone, colour TV with satellite, and radio. There is a spacious cocktail lounge and a restaurant serving the best of modern and classic cuisine. Local attractions include the Metro Centre, Northumbria National Park, Holy Island and Bamburgh Castle.
Single from £52.50, double from £89.50.

AA
★★★

Publisher's note

While every effort is made to ensure accuracy, we regret that FHG Guides cannot accept responsibility for errors, misrepresentations or omissions in our entries or any consequences thereof. Prices in particular should be checked.
We will follow up complaints but cannot act as arbiters or agents for either party.

A useful index of towns/counties appears on pages 347-350

Crewe

Cheshire

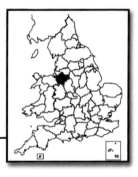

Cheshire - soak in the atmosphere of the historic city of Chester, created by an abundance of black-and-white buildings set in a circuit of glorious city walls, the most complete in the country. Chester's crowning glory is the 13th century Rows – two tiers of shops running along the main streets, offering a unique and sophisticated shopping experience. A leisurely walk along the finest city walls in Britain will take you past most of the city's delights like the stunning Eastgate Clock and the 1000-year-old Cathedral. The lush countryside surrounding Chester is peppered with stately homes, award-winning gardens and chic market towns featuring characteristic black-and-white half-timbered buildings. Tatton Park near Knutsford is one of Britain's finest Georgian manors, with acres of parklands and formal gardens, a perfect attraction to enjoy in every season, and the host of the RHS Flower Show in July. Or visit Arley Hall and Gardens near Northwich, with its stunning herbaceous borders and Country Fair and Horse Trials in May. For super chic in super villages and towns, breeze into Tarporley, Nantwich, Knutsford and Wilmslow where sophisticated shopping, fine cuisine and contemporary pleasures ensure an afternoon of indulgence and fine delights, with food and drink festivals being held throughout the year.

symbols

	Totally non-smoking		Pets Welcome
	Children Welcome	SB	Short Breaks
	Suitable for Disabled Guests		Licensed

Cumbria

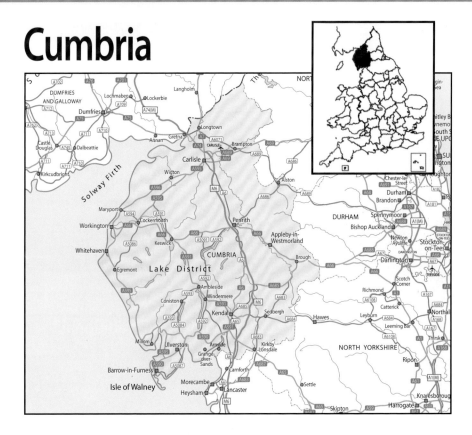

Cumbria - The Lake District is often described as the most beautiful corner

of England, and it's easy to see why 15 million visitors head here every year. It is a place of unrivalled beauty, with crystal clear lakes, bracken-covered mountains, peaceful forests, quiet country roads and miles of stunning coastline.

At the heart of Cumbria is the Lake District National Park. Each of the lakes that make up the area has its own charm and personality: Windermere, England's longest lake, is surrounded by rolling hills; Derwentwater and Ullswater are circled by craggy fells; England's deepest lake, Wastwater, is dominated by high mountains including the country's highest, Scafell Pike. For those who want to tackle the great outdoors, Cumbria offers everything from rock climbing to fell walking and from canoeing to horse riding – all among stunning scenery.

Cumbria has many delightful market towns, historic houses and beautiful gardens such as Holker Hall with its 25 acres of award-winning grounds. There are many opportunities to sample local produce, such as Cumbrian fell-bred lamb, Cumberland Sausage, and trout and salmon plucked fresh from nearby lakes and rivers.

Cumbria is a county of contrasts with a rich depth of cultural and historical interest in addition to stunning scenery. Compact and accessible, it can offer something for every taste.

When making enquiries please mention FHG GUIDES

Ambleside, Appleby-in-Westmorland, Bowness-on-Windermere

Cockermouth, Gilsland

symbols

	Totally non-smoking		Pets Welcome
	Children Welcome	**SB**	Short Breaks
	Suitable for Disabled Guests		Licensed

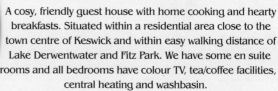

SB

♉

Book with this advert and claim a FREE dessert per resident at dinner (conditions apply).

THE BRITANNIA INN

Elterwater, Langdale, Cumbria LA22 9HP
Tel: 015394 37210

A 500 year-old quintessential Lakeland Inn nestled in the centre of the picturesque village of Elterwater amidst the imposing fells of the Langdale Valley. Comfortable, high quality en suite double and twin-bedded rooms. Dogs welcome. Relax in the oak-beamed Bars or Dining Room whilst sampling local real ales and dishes from our extensive menu of fresh, home-cooked food using lots of Cumbrian produce. *Quiz Night most Sundays.*

Enquire about our Mid-Week Special Offer of three nights B&B for the price of two.

www.britinn.co.uk • e-mail: info@britinn.co.uk

Nestling in the delightful hamlet of Troutbeck, in the heart of the Lake District National Park and with spectacular views of the surrounding fells, our charming family-run Inn has everything you need for a relaxing break, and to sample everything the Lakes have to offer.

We have seven delightful bedrooms, all en suite, and three beautiful self-catering cottages.

Our restaurant is renowned for its excellent home made food which is all sourced locally, and for our fine wines and real ales.

VisitBritain ★★★ Inn/ ★★★★ SC

The Troutbeck Inn, Troutbeck, Penrith, Cumbria CA11 0SJ • Tel: 017684 83635
e-mail: info@thetroutbeckinn.co.uk • www.thetroutbeckinn.co.uk

Visit the FHG website
www.holidayguides.com
for details of the wide choice of accommodation
featured in the full range of FHG titles

Penrith

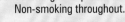

Lancashire

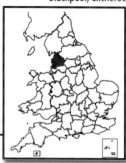

The Berkswell Hotel is a family-run licensed hotel near to Blackpool's Pleasure Beach, South Pier, Sandcastle, Lido and Airport. There are five double, one twin, one family and one single bedrooms.

Berkswell Hotel
8 Withnell Road, South Shore,
Blackpool FY4 1HF
Tel: 01253 341374
**   0800 977 4723**
www.berkswellhotel.co.uk

★★★
GUEST HOUSE

- All rooms en-suite
- Colour TV/DVDs (library of DVDs to borrow).
- Hairdryers
- Tea & coffee facilities
- Good home cooking
- Tables for two
- Special diets catered for
- Car park • Late keys
- Full central heating
- Double glazed throughout
- Comfortable bar

Rakefoot Farm
Chaigley, Near Clitheroe BB7 3LY
VisitBritain ★★★★
VisitBritain ★★★/★★★★
Tel: (Chipping) 01995 61332 or 07889 279063 • Fax: 01995 61296
e-mail: info@rakefootfarm.co.uk • website: www.rakefootfarm.co.uk
Family farm in the beautiful countryside of the Ribble Valley in the peaceful Forest of Bowland, with panoramic views. Ideally placed for touring Coast, Dales and Lakes. 9 miles M6 Junction 31a. Superb walks, golf and horse riding nearby, or visit pretty villages and factory shops. Warm welcome whether on holiday or business, refreshments on arrival.

BED AND BREAKFAST or SELF-CATERING in 17th century farmhouse and traditional stone barn conversion. Wood-burning stoves, central heating, exposed beams and stonework. Most bedrooms en suite, some ground floor. Excellent home cooked meals, pubs/restaurants nearby. Garden and patios. Dogs by arrangement. Laundry. **Past winner of NWTB Silver Award for Self-catering Holiday of the Year.**

B&B £25 - £32.50pppn sharing, £25 - £37.50pn single
S/C four properties (3 can be internally interlinked)
£111 - £695 per property per week. Short breaks available.

symbols

Totally non-smoking		Pets Welcome
Children Welcome	**SB**	Short Breaks
Suitable for Disabled Guests	♀	Licensed

Sandy Brook Farm,
52 Wyke Cop Road, Scarisbrick, Southport
PR8 5LR • 01704 880337

Bill and Wendy Core offer a homely, friendly atmosphere at Sandy Brook, a small working farm situated three-and-a-half miles from the seaside resort of Southport and five miles from the historic town of Ormskirk. Motorways are easily accessible, and the Lake District, Trough of Bowland, Blackpool and North Wales are within easy reach. Six en suite bedrooms with colour TV and tea/coffee making facilities. Room available for disabled guests. Open all year except Christmas. Bed and Breakfast from £22.50. Reductions for children. Weekly terms on request.

ETC ★★★

e-mail: sandybrookfarm@lycos.co.uk
www.sandybrookfarm.co.uk

Merseyside

Southport

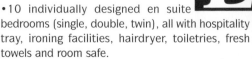

Publisher's note

England

Self-Catering

Whitsand Bay Self Catering Holidays, page 144

Chapel Cottages, St Tudy, Cornwall, page 146

Other specialised holiday guides from **FHG**

PUBS & INNS OF BRITAIN

COUNTRY HOTELS OF BRITAIN

WEEKEND & SHORT BREAKS IN BRITAIN & IRELAND

THE GOLF GUIDE WHERE TO PLAY, WHERE TO STAY

PETS WELCOME!

SELF-CATERING HOLIDAYS IN BRITAIN

BED & BREAKFAST STOPS IN BRITAIN

CARAVAN & CAMPING HOLIDAYS IN BRITAIN

FAMILY BREAKS IN BRITAIN

Published annually: available in all good bookshops or direct from the publisher:

FHG Guides, Abbey Mill Business Centre, Seedhill, Paisley PA1 1TJ

Tel: 0141 887 0428 • Fax: 0141 889 7204

e-mail: admin@fhguides.co.uk • www.holidayguides.com

Cornwall

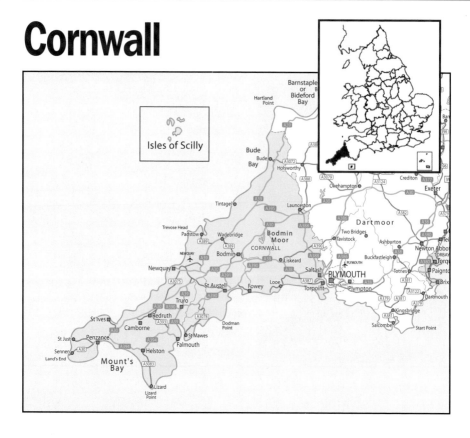

Isles of Scilly

Cornish Seaview Cottages

SB

14 gorgeous holiday properties on the North Cornish coast. Sleeping from 2 – 20. In fantastic locations with great views. Ideal for walking the coastal paths and accessing the local beaches. Pets are welcome at most and we pride ourselves on our personal service and welcome. Tastefully furnished and equipped to a high standard with all the comforts required for a relaxing holiday.

www.cornishseaviewcottages.co.uk
Tel: 01428 723819
e-mail: enquiries@cornishseaviewcottages.co.uk

• *enclosed garden* • *walks nearby*
• *£20 per pet*

Please note

All the information in this book is given in good faith in the belief that it is correct. However, the publishers cannot guarantee the facts given in these pages, neither are they responsible for changes in policy, ownership or terms that may take place after the date of going to press. Readers should always satisfy themselves that the facilities they require are available and that the terms, if quoted, still apply.

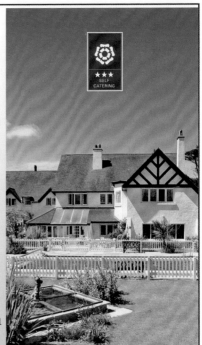

Fowey, Helford Estuary, Helston

Liskeard

CUTKIVE WOOD HOLIDAY LODGES

Nestling in the heart of a peaceful family-owned country estate are six well-equipped comfortable cedar-clad lodges. Set on the edge of ancient bluebell woods with lovely rural views, you can relax and enjoy yourself in this tranquil and idyllic setting. Help with the animals, explore the woods and fields, fun play area. So much for everyone to see and do – memorable beaches, wonderful coasts, walk the moors, inspiring gardens and Eden, theme attractions, historic gems. Dogs welcome. Ideally situated to enjoy coast and country holidays whatever the time of year.

St Ive, Liskeard, Cornwall PL14 3ND • Tel: 01579 362216
www.cutkivewood.co.uk • e-mail: holidays@cutkivewood.co.uk

Boturnell Barns
Cornwall

Really dog-friendly self-catering accommodation, set in 25 acres of fields and woodland between Looe and Bodmin.
No limit on number of pets.
Well equipped. Linen included.
Dog creche. Enclosed garden. Exercise area. Walks nearby.

Sue Jewell, Boturnell Farm Cottages St Pinnock, Liskeard PL14 4QS
Tel: 01579 320880
e-mail: sue@dogs-holiday.co.uk www.dogs-holiday.co.uk

SB

Looe

Penquite Country Cottages
Duloe, Near Looe PL14 4QG

Four spacious and comfortable one-bedroom cottages for couples, or just one. Set in tranquil surroundings and enjoying outstanding views, Penquite offers real peace and quiet. Woodland walks from your front door, and within easy distance of the moors and coast, we are well situated for all that Cornwall has to offer. Fully equipped; heating, electricity, bedding and towels all included.

Well behaved dogs most welcome.
No children.

Please contact
Martin and Wendy Welch
for further information/brochure on
01503 220260
or e-mail:
stay@penquitecountrycottages.co.uk
See us at
www.penquitecountrycottages.co.uk

The Perfect Cornish Country Cottage

THE OLD BARN is located in a small hamlet of renovated farm buildings, situated in the hills above the pretty coastal town of Looe, South East Cornwall. It enjoys magnificent views across the valley and has a completely enclosed garden. Within easy reach of the coast, the Eden Project, and the Lost Gardens of Heligan.
• Sleeps 6.

For further details, ring
Carolyn & Richard - 01503 265739
www.oldbarnholidays.net

TREMAINE GREEN
for MEMORABLE HOLIDAYS

"A beautiful private hamlet" of 11 traditional cosy Cornish craftsmen's cottages between **Looe** and **Polperro**. Clean, comfortable and well equipped, with a warm friendly atmosphere, for pets with 2 to 8 people. Set in award-winning grounds, only 12 miles from the **Eden Project** with country and coastal walks nearby. Pets £18 pw; owners from only **£123**.

SB

• Towels, Linen, Electric & Hot Water included • Dishwashers in larger cottages • Launderette • Kid's Play Area • Games Room • Tennis Court • TV/DVDs• Cots & Highchairs • Pubs & Restaurants in easy walking distance • Activities Area

Mr & Mrs J Spreckley, Tremaine Green Country Cottages, Pelynt, Near Looe, Cornwall PL13 2LT
www.tremainegreen.co.uk • e-mail: stay@tremainegreen.co.uk • Tel: (01503) 220333

symbols

⊘	Totally non-smoking	🐕	Pets Welcome
🐎	Children Welcome	**SB**	Short Breaks
♿	Suitable for Disabled Guests	⏶	Licensed

Newquay, Padstow

Visit the FHG website
www.holidayguides.com

for details of the wide choice of accommodation
featured in the full range of FHG titles

SB

CHAPEL COTTAGES   ST TUDY

Four traditional cottages, sleeping 2 to 5, in a quiet farming area. Ideal for the spectacular north coast, Bodmin Moor, and the Eden Project. Comfortable and well-equipped. Garden and private parking. Rental £160 to £445 per week. Also two smaller cottages for couples at Hockadays, near Blisland - converted from a 17th century barn in a quiet farming hamlet. Rental £160 to £345 per week. Shop and pub/restaurant within walking distance. Regretfully, no pets. Brochure available.

Mrs M. Pestell, 'Hockadays', Tregenna, Blisland PL30 4QJ • Tel: 01208 850146
www.hockadays.co.uk

Devon

Devon is unique, with two different coastlines: bare rugged cliffs, white pebble beaches, stretches of golden sands, and the Jurassic Coast, England's first natural World Heritage Site. Glorious countryside: green rolling hills, bustling market towns and villages, thatched, white-washed cottages and traditional Devon longhouses. Wild and wonderful moorland: Dartmoor, in the south, embraces wild landscapes and picture-postcard villages; Exmoor in the north combines breathtaking, rugged coastline with wild heather moorland. Step back in time and discover historic cities, myths and legends, seafaring characters like Drake and Raleigh, and settings for novels by Agatha Christie and Conan Doyle.

Devon is home to an amazing and diverse range of birds. Enjoy special organised birdwatching trips, perhaps on board a RSPB Avocet Cruise or a vintage tram. Devon is the walking county of the South West – imagine drifts of bluebells lit by dappled sunlight, the smell of new mown hay, the sound of the sea, crisp country walks followed by a roaring fire and hot 'toddies'! If pedal power is your choice, you will discover exciting off-road cycling, leisurely afternoon rides, and challenging long distance routes such as the Granite Way along Dartmoor, the Grand Western Canal and the coastal Exmouth to Budleigh Circuit.

Please mention 500 Great Places to Stay
when making enquiries about accommodation featured in these pages

Ashburton, Axminster, Barnstaple, Bigbury-on-Sea

Wooder Manor

**Widecombe-in-the-Moor
Near Ashburton TQ13 7TR**

Cottages and converted coach house, on 170-acre working family farm nestled in the picturesque valley of Widecombe, surrounded by unspoilt woodland, moors and granite tors. Half-a-mile from village with post office, general stores, inn with dining room, church and National Trust Information Centre. Excellent centre for touring Devon with a variety of places to visit and exploring Dartmoor by foot or on horseback. Accommodation is clean and well equipped with colour TV, central heating, laundry room. Children welcome. Large gardens and courtyard for easy parking. Open all year, so take advantage of off-season reduced rates. Short Breaks also available. Two properties suitable for disabled visitors. Colour brochure .

Tel & Fax: 01364 621391

e-mail: angela@woodermanor.com
website: www.woodermanor.com

🏇 🐕 SB ♿

Cider Room Cottage Hasland Farm, Membury, Axminster.

This delightfully converted thatched cider barn, with exposed beams, adjoins main farmhouse overlooking the outstanding beauty of the orchards, pools and pastureland, and is ideally situated for touring Devon, Dorset and Somerset. Bathing, golf and tennis at Lyme Regis and many places of interest locally, including Wildlife Park, donkey sanctuary and Forde Abbey. Membury Village, with its post office and stores, trout farm, and church is one mile away. The accommodation is of the highest standard with the emphasis on comfort. Two double rooms; shower room and toilet; sitting/diningroom with colour TV; kitchen with electric cooker, microwave, washing machine, fridge. Linen supplied. Pets by arrangement. Car essential. Open all year. No smoking. Terms from £180 to £350.   SAE, please, to

Mrs Pat Steele, Hasland Farm, Membury, Axminster EX13 7JF
davidsteele887@btinternet.com • www.ciderroomcottage.com

Tel: 01404 881558

🚭 🏇 🐕 SB

An Exmoor Hideaway
MARTINHOE CLEAVE COTTAGES

Overlooking the beautiful Heddon Valley and close to the dramatic coast of the Exmoor National Park, these delightful cottages, equipped to a very high standard throughout, offer perfect rural tranquillity.
Open all year • Sleep 1-2

Martinhoe, Parracombe, Barnstaple, Devon EX31 4PZ
Tel: 01598 763313
e-mail: info@exmoorhideaway.co.uk www.exmoorhideaway.co.uk

🐕 SB

A delightful family working farm, situated on the coast, overlooking the sea and sandy beaches of Bigbury Bay. Farm adjoins golf course and River Avon. Lovely coastal walks. Ideal centre for South Hams and Dartmoor. The spacious wing (sleeps 2/6) comprises half of the farmhouse, and is completely self-contained. All rooms attractively furnished. Large, comfortable lounge overlooking the sea. There are three bedrooms: one family, one double and a bunk bed; two have washbasins. The kitchen/diner has a fridge/freezer, electric cooker, microwave, washing machine and dishwasher. There is a nice garden, ideal for children. Sorry, no smoking. Reduction for two people staying in off peak weeks. Please write or telephone for a brochure. *Jane Tucker.*
www.bigburyholidays.co.uk • *Tel:* 01548 810267

Mount Folly Farm
Bigbury-on-Sea,
Kingsbridge TQ7 4AR

🚭 🏇 🐕 SB

Visit the FHG website
www.holidayguides.com

for details of the wide choice of accommodation

featured in the full range of FHG titles

Brixham

DEVONCOURT
HOLIDAY FLATS

SB

BERRYHEAD ROAD, BRIXHAM, DEVON TQ5 9AB

Devoncourt is a development of 24 self-contained flats, occupying one of the finest positions in Torbay, with unsurpassed views.

At night the lights of Torbay are like a fairyland to be enjoyed from your very own balcony.

EACH FLAT HAS:
Heating
Sea Views over Torbay
Private balcony
Own front door
Separate bathroom and toilet
Separate bedroom
Bed-settee in lounge
Lounge sea views over Marina
Kitchenette - all electric
Private car park
Opposite beach
Colour television
Overlooks lifeboat
Short walk to town centre
Double glazing
Open all year
Mini Breaks October to April

Harbour view from Devoncourt

Tel: 01803 853748
(or 07802 403289 after office hours)
www.devoncourt.info

Northcott Barton Farm Cottage

SB

Beautifully equipped, spotlessly clean three bedroom cottage with large enclosed garden. A walker's and country lover's ideal: for a couple seeking peace and quiet or a family holiday. Very special rates for low season holidays, couples and short breaks. Near golf, riding, Tarka trail and R.H.S. Rosemoor. Character, comfort, beams, log fire, *"Perfick"*. Pets Welcome, no charge.

For availability please contact Sandra Gay,
Northcott Barton, Ashreigney, Chulmleigh, Devon EX18 7PR
Tel/Fax: 01769 520259
e-mail: sandra@northcottbarton.co.uk
www.northcottbarton.co.uk

BONEHAYNE FARM   COTTAGE: CARAVAN: BOARD
COLYTON, DEVON EX24 6SG

SB

- Family 250 acre working farm • Competitive prices
- Spectacular views • South facing luxury caravan
- Cottage with four-poster and central heating
- Four miles to the beach • Five minutes from Colyton
- Spacious lawns/gardens • Laundry room, BBQ, picnic tables
- Good trout fishing, woods to roam, walks

Mrs Gould
Tel: 01404 871396/871416

www.bonehayne.co.uk • e-mail: gould@bonehayne.co.uk

SB

Situated beside the village church, the cottages (sleep 4/5) have been tastefully renovated to maintain the old style of the barn. With panoramic views over the Coly valley, they provide a quiet holiday and offer many interesting walks. Riding stables and ancient monuments are within walking distance. Honiton Golf Course, swimming pool and bowling green are four miles away. Lyme Regis, Sidmouth and Exmouth plus many other quaint scenic coastal resorts and the Jurassic Coast are all within half an hour's drive; situated on the route of the East Devon (Foxglove) Way.

Each cottage has a modern kitchen complete with washing machine and microwave as well as a conventional cooker, comfortable lounge with colour TV and DVD/Digibox, two bedrooms, and bathroom with bath and shower. Central heating • Electricity by £1 meter • Bed linen supplied • New games room • Brochure on request • Bed and Breakfast available at our farmhouse.

Church Approach Cottages
Church Green, Farway, Colyton
Devon EX24 6EQ

For further details please contact: Sheila & Liz Lee
Tel: 01404 871383/871202
e-mail: lizlee@eclipse.co.uk • www.churchapproach.co.uk

Visit the FHG website
www.holidayguides.com
for details of the wide choice of accommodation
featured in the full range of FHG titles

Kingsbridge, Noss Mayo

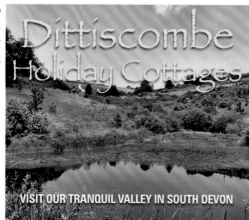

"Perfect location...Perfect bolt hole Such a peaceful and beautiful valley"

Relax in one of our cottages with a woodburner and country views; take a walk along the stunning coastal paths; sample the menus in the excellent local pubs; and enjoy unique shopping in nearby Totnes, Dartmouth and Salcombe.

- Short Breaks off season
  - Open all year

Dittiscombe Holiday Cottages, Slapton Near Kingsbridge, South Devon TQ7 2QF

For more information, prices and availability, please visit our website:

Tel: 01548 521272   **www.dittiscombe.co.uk**

CRAB COTTAGE NOSS MAYO SOUTH DEVON
www.crab-cottage.co.uk
- Charming fisherman's cottage, 50 yards from the quay on the River Yealm
- Watch the boats on the river from the cottage gardens and window seats • Delightful, quiet village in an area of outstanding natural beauty • Fantastic walks, beaches and dog-friendly pubs on the doorstep • Walk across to village shops in Newton Ferrers at low tide
- Close to the South Devon Coastal Path • Sleeps 5

Phone 01425 471372 for a brochure • e-mail: kaspar.gobell@btinternet.com

symbols

  Totally non-smoking   Pets Welcome

  Children Welcome   **SB** Short Breaks

  Suitable for Disabled Guests   Licensed

TOTNES J. and E. Ball, Higher Well Farm and Holiday Park, Stoke Gabriel, Totnes TQ9 6RN (01803 782289).
A quiet secluded farm park welcoming tents, motor caravans and touring caravans. It is less than one mile from the riverside village of Stoke Gabriel and within four miles of Torbay beaches. Central for touring South Devon. Facilities include modern toilet/shower block with dishwashing and family rooms. Electric hook-ups and hard standings. Launderette, shop and payphone.
SB
• Also static caravans to let from £160 per week or £22 per night.
ETC ★★★★

Westward Ho!, Woolacombe

WEST PUSEHILL FARM COTTAGES

Resident proprietors, The Violet Family have been welcoming visitors to West Pusehill Farm for over twenty years, and many return time and time again.

Ideal for family summer holidays, restful spring/winter breaks, or a perfect base to explore Devon's outstanding coast and countryside and many outdoor activities.

West Pusehill Farm Cottages not only give you the freedom and independence of a self-catering holiday, but the local area offers a wide range of excellent restaurants and cafes, so your holiday can be enjoyed by every member of the family.

❖ Located in an Area of Outstanding Natural Beauty
❖ Eleven sympathetically converted cottages
❖ BBQ area
❖ Children's playground
❖ On-site heated outdoor pool
❖ Laundry room
❖ Golf, fishing, walking, exploring, shopping
❖ Family attractions

West Pusehill Farm
Westward Ho!
North Devon EX39 5AH
Tel: 01237 475638/474622
e-mail: info@wpfcottages.co.uk
www.wpfcottages.co.uk

Resthaven
Holiday Flats

The Esplanade, Woolacombe, Devon EX34 7DJ

On the sea front overlooking the beautiful Combesgate beach. Fantastic views of Morte Point and the coastline.
★ Two self contained flats, sleeping 5 & 9.
★ Family, double and bunk bedrooms all with washbasins.
★ All-electric kitchens. Electricity on £1 meter.
★ Bathrooms with bath & shower.
★ Colour TVs with video and DVD players.
★ Free parking, lighting, hot water and laundry.
★ Terms £160 to £900 per week.
Contact Brian Watts for details and brochure.
Tel: 01271 870248
e-mail: rhflats@orange.net

Publisher's note

While every effort is made to ensure accuracy, we regret that FHG Guides cannot accept responsibility for errors, misrepresentations or omissions in our entries or any consequences thereof. Prices in particular should be checked.

We will follow up complaints but cannot act as arbiters or agents for either party.

Dorset

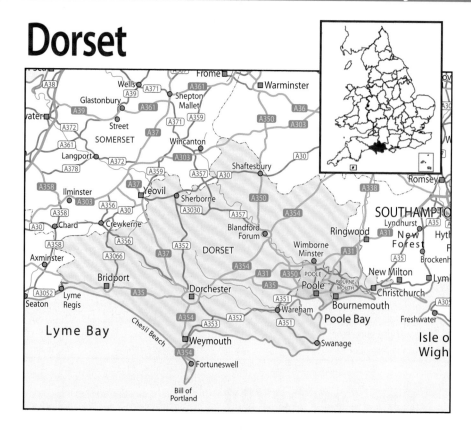

A useful index of towns/counties appears on pages 347-350

Blandford Forum, Burton Bradstock, Lyme Regis, Powerstock/Bridport

Gloucestershire

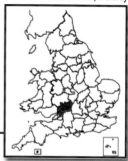

SB

Cosy, well equipped, self-contained apartment with open aspects, attached to the farmhouse of a 100 acre livestock farm. Situated on the eastern outskirts of Cheltenham, on the edge of the Cotswold Escarpment. Comfortably furnished, with full central heating and plenty of parking space. Electricity and bed linen included in rental. Ideal position for visiting the lovely Regency town of Cheltenham and the mellow villages of the Cotswolds.

Sorry, no pets allowed. Non-smoking.
Terms from £160 to £230 per week. ETC ★★★

Mr & Mrs J. Close, Coxhorne Farm, London Road, Charlton Kings,Cheltenham GL52 6UY
Tel: 01242 236599 • e-mail: sue_close2003@yahoo.co.uk

SB

Two Springbank, 37 Hopton Road, Upper Cam GL11 5PD

Fully equipped mid-terraced cottage (sleeps 4 + cot) in pleasant village about one mile from Dursley which has a swimming pool and sports centre.
Superb base for Cotswold Way, touring Severn Vale and Forest of Dean.
Few miles from Slimbridge Wildfowl Trust, Berkeley Castle and Westonbirt Arboretum and within easy reach of Gloucester, Bristol, Bath and Cirencester.
Ground floor: sitting room with TV/video and electric fire, dining area, fitted kitchen with fridge/freezer, electric cooker and microwave. Utility room with washing machine; lawn and patio. **First floor:** two bedrooms (one double, one twin),bathroom with shower.
Linen and towels included, also cot and highchair if required. Rates from £198-£246 per week (low season), £246-£276 (high season). Includes electricity. • Off-peak breaks (3 nights) from £120 to £168.
Sorry no pets or smoking
Mrs F.A. Jones, 32 Everlands, Cam, Dursley, Gloucs GL11 5NL • 01453 543047
e-mail: freedaj2sb37@btinternet.com

---

symbols

 Totally non-smoking

 Children Welcome

⚿ Suitable for Disabled Guests

 Pets Welcome

SB Short Breaks

 Licensed

Bath

Somerset

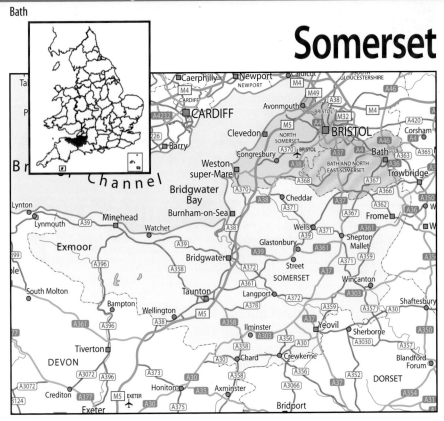

Situated just four miles north of Bath and within a few miles of Lacock, Castle Combe, Tetbury and the Cotswolds. The 17th century farm buildings have been converted into luxury self-catering cottages with well equipped kitchens. Ample car parking. Pets welcome. Separate laundry room and all bed linen, towels etc. included. B&B also available in warm and cosy 17th century farmhouse.

Toghill House Farm, Toghill, Wick, Near Bath BS30 5RT
Tel: 01225 891261 • Fax: 01225 892128 • www.toghillhousefarm.co.uk

Publisher's note

Coast Road, Brean Sands, Somerset TA8 2QZ
Tel: 01278 751346 • Fax: 01278 751683

FREEPHONE 08000 190322
www.beachsideholidaypark.co.uk

SB

• Chalets and Caravan holiday homes on quiet park
• Direct access to beach • Pets from £4 per night
• Full facilities • Colour television • Cafe/Bar
• Golf courses nearby • Free brochure

TAMARACK LODGE, CHARD

This luxurious, traditionally styled, ranch house-type log cabin enjoys extensive views of the delightful Yarty Valley. It was purpose-built to provide self-catering holiday accommodation for both able-bodied and disabled people, and sleeps up to eight. It is very wheelchair-friendly, and has two of the three double bedrooms on the ground floor, and a large ground floor wc/shower room.

SB

Tamarack Lodge is situated on a family-run beef and sheep farm in the beautiful Blackdown Hills, an Area of Outstanding Natural Beauty near the Somerset/Devon border.

NATIONAL ACCESSIBLE SCHEME LEVEL 1.

Matthew Sparks, Fyfett Farm, Otterford, Chard TA20 3QP • 01823 601270
e-mail: matthew.sparks@tamaracklodge.co.uk • www.tamaracklodge.co.uk

Looking for Holiday Accommodation?

FHG
K·U·P·E·R·A·R·D

for details of hundreds of properties throughout the UK, visit our website

www.holidayguides.com

Duddings
COUNTRY COTTAGES

VB ★ ★ ★ ★

SB

As resident owners, we personally guarantee immaculate presentation of cottages on arrival. Each cottage has tasteful decor with matching, highest quality fabrics and is fully central heated. Amenities include comfortable lounges with colour TV/video/DVD, fully fitted modern kitchens with fridge-freezer, cooker and microwave. Our facilities include heated indoor pool, hard tennis court, putting green, pool and table tennis, trampoline, football net and play centre. Trout stream in 8.5 acres for fishing or picnics. Families and pets welcome, walking, riding, beaches nearby. Short breaks available off season, open all year. Full details and plans of the cottages together with up to date prices and availablity can be found on our website, or please call for brochure.

Thatched longhouse and 12 cottages for 2-12 persons, beautifully converted from old stone barns and stables. Original beams and exposed stonework retain the character of the buildings. Two miles from the picturesque village of Dunster in the Exmoor National Park.

Luxury Cottages

Indoor Heated Pool

Tennis Court

Colour brochure from Duddings Timberscombe Dunster, Somerset TA24 7TB

Telephone: 01643 841123
www.duddings.co.uk
e-mail: richard@duddings.co.uk

Riscombe Farm Holiday Cottages – Exmoor National Park

SB

Four charming self-catering stone cottages converted from barns surrounding an attractive courtyard with stables. Very comfortable, with log fires and equipped to a high standard, sleeping 2-6. Peaceful, relaxing location beside the River Exe in the centre of Exmoor National Park. Excellent walking and riding country in the valleys, across the moors or along the spectacular coast.

One and a half miles from Exford Village.
Dogs and horses welcome. Stabling provided.

Open all year   VisitBritain ★★★★

Leone & Brian Martin,
Riscombe Farm, Exford,
Somerset TA24 7NH
Tel: 01643 831480
www.riscombe.co.uk *(with vacancy info.)*

Wintershead Farm, Simonsbath, Exmoor, Somerset TA24 7LF

Wintershead is ideal for holiday makers looking for a relaxing break away from the crowded coastal resorts, occupying a unique location with breathtaking views. Five quality stone cottages converted from original farm buildings offer all the comforts of home, yet are not far from all the local attractions: the famous Doone valley and Oare church, Lynton, Lynmouth and Porlock, and the sleepy villages of Dunster, Dulverton and Exford. There is excellent fishing locally on the Barle, Exe, East and West Lyn rivers, or, if you want to be closer to nature, there are riding stables nearby; if you enjoy walking, the Two Moors Way is on the doorstep. The golden beaches of Croyde, Saunton Sands and Woolacombe are a short and pleasant drive away, passing quaint fishing villages, Ilfracombe, Combe Martin and the historic town of Barnstaple. If you would like an unforgettable day out, the Somerset Levels, Cheddar Caves and Wookey Hole are within easy driving distance, as are the Eden Project and the Lost Gardens of Heligan.

Wintershead is an ideal base from which to explore the beautiful West Country. Easy to find – yet so hard to leave.
Colour brochure available. Telephone Jane Styles on 01643 831222 or look at www.wintershead.co.uk

Please note

All the information in this book is given in good faith in the belief that it is correct. However, the publishers cannot guarantee the facts given in these pages, neither are they responsible for changes in policy, ownership or terms that may take place after the date of going to press. Readers should always satisfy themselves that the facilities they require are available and that the terms, if quoted, still apply.

A useful index of towns/counties appears on pages 347-350

Muchelney Ham Farm
Muchelney Ham, Langport TA10 0DJ

Self-catering cottages built in traditional style adjoining farmhouse. Double and family bedrooms, en suite. Large kitchen/diningroom. One further bathroom downstairs. Stable cottage has a downstairs bedroom. Electricity by coin meter. Linen included in price.

Open all year

Weekly terms from £160 to £420, or from £125 to £300.

Bed & Breakfast accommodation also available.

Tel: 01458 250737

English Tourism Council

★★★
SELF CATERING

www.muchelneyhamfarm.co.uk

Other specialised holiday guides from **FHG**

PUBS & INNS OF BRITAIN

COUNTRY HOTELS OF BRITAIN

WEEKEND & SHORT BREAKS IN BRITAIN & IRELAND

THE GOLF GUIDE WHERE TO PLAY, WHERE TO STAY

PETS WELCOME!

SELF-CATERING HOLIDAYS IN BRITAIN

BED & BREAKFAST STOPS IN BRITAIN

CARAVAN & CAMPING HOLIDAYS IN BRITAIN

FAMILY BREAKS IN BRITAIN

Published annually: available in all good bookshops or direct from the publisher:

FHG Guides, Abbey Mill Business Centre, Seedhill, Paisley PA1 1TJ

Tel: 0141 887 0428 • Fax: 0141 889 7204

e-mail: admin@fhguides.co.uk • www.holidayguides.com

Please note

All the information in this book is given in good faith in the belief that it is correct. However, the publishers cannot guarantee the facts given in these pages, neither are they responsible for changes in policy, ownership or terms that may take place after the date of going to press. Readers should always satisfy themselves that the facilities they require are available and that the terms, if quoted, still apply.

Wiltshire

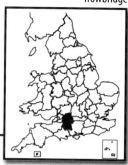

SB

John and Elizabeth Moody
Gaston Farm, Holt,
Trowbridge BA14 6QA
Tel: 01225 782203

The self-contained accommodation is part of a farmhouse, dating from the 16th century, on the edge of the village of Holt with views across open farmland. Within 10 miles of Bath, Bradford-on-Avon two miles, Lacock eight miles. Private fishing on River Avon available.

The apartment consists of a large lounge/dining room with open fire and sofa which converts into a double bed; two generously proportioned bedrooms upstairs, one twin-bedded, one with a double bed, both with washbasins; a separate toilet (downstairs); a large kitchen in the single storey wing, fitted with light oak finish units, electric cooker, microwave, refrigerator and automatic washing machine; shower room which opens off the kitchen. Electricity extra.

Off-road parking. Choice of pubs in village.
Terms £200 to £225. Brochure and further details available.

Looking for Holiday Accommodation?

for details of hundreds of properties throughout the UK, visit our website

www.holidayguides.com

Olney

Buckinghamshire

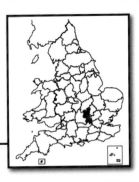

Old Stone Barn

Mr & Mrs Garry Pibworth,
Home Farm, Warrington,
Olney MK46 4HN
Tel: 01234 711655
Fax: 01234 711855

The Old Stone Barn is peacefully positioned on an arable farm 1½ miles from the beautiful market town of Olney where there is a wide variety of shops, cafes, bars and restaurants. The accommodation is a charming combination of old character and modern facilities, and consists of 7 spacious self-contained apartments (sleep 1-6), centrally heated and equipped with colour TV and payphone. Linen and towels are provided, and there is a laundry room with washing machines and a tumble dryer. Computer room and wifi available.

Guests can relax in the gardens, make use of the outdoor heated swimming pool, or take day trips to Oxford, Cambridge, London or the Cotswolds.
Terms from £240 to £560 per week.
e-mail: info@oldstonebarn.co.uk
www.oldstonebarn.co.uk

SB

The Old Stone Barn
HOME FARM

★★★★
SELF
CATERING

FHG Guides
publish a large range of well-known accommodation guides.
We will be happy to send you details or you can use the order form
at the back of this book.

Please note

All the information in this book is given in good faith in the belief that it is correct.

However, the publishers cannot guarantee the facts given in these pages, neither are

they responsible for changes in policy, ownership or terms that may take place after the

date of going to press. Readers should always satisfy themselves that the facilities they

require are available and that the terms, if quoted, still apply.

Isle of Wight

symbols

	Totally non-smoking		Pets Welcome
	Children Welcome	**SB**	Short Breaks
	Suitable for Disabled Guests		Licensed

BONCHURCH. Ashcliff Holiday Apartment, Bonchurch PO38 1NT.
Idyllic and secluded position in the picturesque seaside village of Bonchurch. Self-contained, ground floor apartment adjoining Victorian house, set in large south-facing gardens with sea views and sheltered by a thickly wooded cliff. Large, private car park.
• Sleeps 2. • Dogs very welcome.
ETC ★★★
For free brochure telephone: 01983 853919.

Creek Gardens

Nestled in a tranquil setting overlooking the picturesque Wootton Creek. These high quality, well equipped holiday apartments and cottages are ideally located for all of the Isle of Wight's many attractions and sandy beaches.

Close to Cowes, host to sailing regattas every summer weekend, or for just enjoying a wealth of outdoor activities including walking, riding, cycling, fishing, exploring, or relaxing and soaking in the wonderful scenery.

**Creek Gardens, New Road, Ryde,
Isle of Wight PO33 4JX
Tel: 01983 883100
enquiries@creekgardens.co.uk**

www.creekgardens.co.uk

SB

Looking for Holiday Accommodation?

FHG

for details of hundreds of properties throughout the UK, visit our website

www.holidayguides.com

Kent

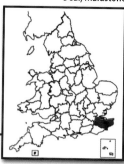

Hidden Gem
59 Gladstone Road, Deal, Kent CT14 7ET

A serene and luxuriously furnished and equipped one bedroom bungalow, with gas central heating, a secure private garden and off-street parking. Situated in a delightful side street next to Deal Castle, the beach, the lively and picturesque seaside town of Deal and endless beach and country walks.

Sleeps 2 • No Smoking • Pets Welcome free

For details please tel Lucy on: 07590 756833 or email via the website www.selfcatering-deal.co.uk

Apple Pye Self-Catering Cottage

Cottage on farm set in 45 acres, surrounded by beautiful rolling Kentish countryside. Well away from the road and next to the farmhouse B&B, it is only 10 minutes' drive from M20, J8. Central location for visiting Kent's many attractions, 6 miles from Leeds Castle, Canterbury half-hour drive, Dover one hour's drive, London one and a quarter hours by train. Sleeps four. One double room en suite, one twin with own shower room; living room/kitchen/dining room with washer/dryer, fridge/freezer, electric cooker, microwave, TV, DVD, wireless broadband. Full Central heating. Garden and patio. Suitable for disabled. Rent £285-£465 per week. B&B also available.

Mr & Mrs Leat, Apple Pye Cottage, Bramley Knowle Farm, Eastwood Road, Ulcombe, Maidstone, Kent ME17 1ET
Tel: 01622 858878 • E-mail: diane@bramleyknowlefarm.co.uk • www.bramleyknowlefarm.co.uk

symbols

	Totally non-smoking		Pets Welcome
	Children Welcome	**SB**	Short Breaks
	Suitable for Disabled Guests		Licensed

Alfrison

Sussex

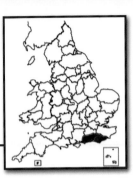

East Sussex

Mrs G. Burgess
Polhills
Arlington, Polegate
East Sussex BN26 6SB
01323 870004
sarahfield@tiscali.co.uk

Idyllically situated on shore of reservoir and edge of Sussex Downs within easy reach of the sea. Self Contained wing of 17th century cottage (approached by own drive along the water's edge) available for self-catering holidays from April to October (inclusive). Fly fishing for trout can be arranged during season. Accommodation consists of two double bedrooms; tiled bathroom. Lounge with colour TV; large well-fitted kitchen with fridge freezer, electric cooker, microwave, washing machine; dining room with put-u-up settee; sun lounge. Central heating. Linen supplied. Most rooms contain a wealth of oak beams.
Car essential. Ample parking. Shops two miles.
Golf, hill climbing locally. Sea eight miles.
Weekly terms from £345 to £390 (electricity included).

Please note

All the information in this book is given in good faith in the belief that it is correct. However, the publishers cannot guarantee the facts given in these pages, neither are they responsible for changes in policy, ownership or terms that may take place after the date of going to press. Readers should always satisfy themselves that the facilities they require are available and that the terms, if quoted, still apply.

SB

Norfolk

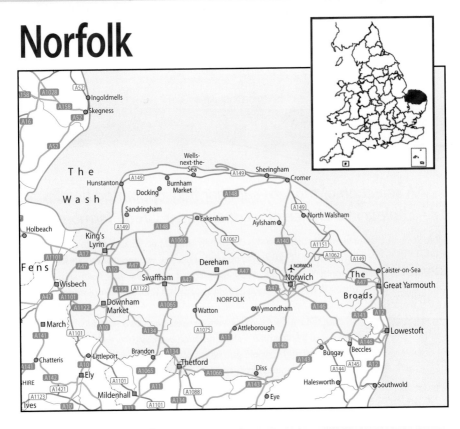

Visit the FHG website

www.holidayguides.com

for details of the wide choice of accommodation

featured in the full range of FHG titles

symbols

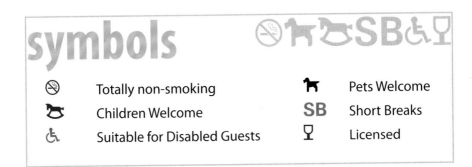

⊘	Totally non-smoking	🐕	Pets Welcome
🐎	Children Welcome	**SB**	Short Breaks
♿	Suitable for Disabled Guests	♉	Licensed

SB

The Holiday Estate with a difference

Winterton Valley Holidays

A selection of modern superior fully appointed holiday chalets in a choice of locations near Great Yarmouth.

No straight lines of identical chalets on this delightfully landscaped 35 acre estate of holiday homes. It has private access to Winterton's fine sandy beaches, with no main roads for children to cross. A wonderful place for a real away from it all holiday, very quiet and yet only 8 miles from Gt Yarmouth. Both the beach and valley are ideal for dog walking, and pets are very welcome.

There are no shops, amusements or clubs on the site. The village of Winterton is a short distance away, with its well stocked stores and 300 year old pub which serves excellent food and drink at the bar or in the family room and garden.

Chalets are privately owned, sleep up to 6 people and each is of individual style. All have open plan lounge and dining areas adjoining the kitchens. Electric heating and TV. Kitchens are all equipped with an electric cooker, microwave and fridge. Bathrooms have a full size bath, wash basin and WC. Most chalets have a shower over the bath.

All chalets have two bedrooms which have a double bed in one room and either twin beds or bunk beds in the second bedroom. You are asked to supply your own bed linen: duvet covers, bottom sheets, pillow cases, towels and tea towels, but these can be supplied for hire if required. Pets are very welcome in most chalets at a small additional fee.

For those wanting a livelier holiday we also have chalets at nearby **California Sands.**

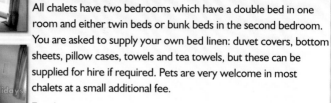

**For colour brochure please ring
01493 377175 or write to
15 Kingston Avenue,
Caister-on-Sea, Norfolk NR30 5ET**
www.wintertonvalleyholidays.co.uk

The Timbers,
The Lane, Winterton-on-Sea

Comfortable, well-furnished ground floor flat in timber cottage, situated in quiet seaside village, just eight miles north of Great Yarmouth. Sandy beach and sand dunes (Nature Reserve) for pleasant walks. Three miles from Norfolk Broads for boating and fishing. Flat is carpeted throughout and fully equipped for self-catering family holidays. Double, twin and single room. Bed linen provided, and maid service twice a week. Attractive beamed sittingroom with colour TV and DVD. Secluded garden.

- *Car parking* • *Sleeps 5 + cot .*
- *Ideal for children* • *Pets welcome*
- *Available May-Sep.* • *From £250 per week*

Please contact: Miss Isherwood, 80 Hillside Gardens, Barnet, Hertfordshire EN5 2NL Tel: 0208 441 3493)
www.winterton-on-sea.net/business/thetimbers

Suffolk

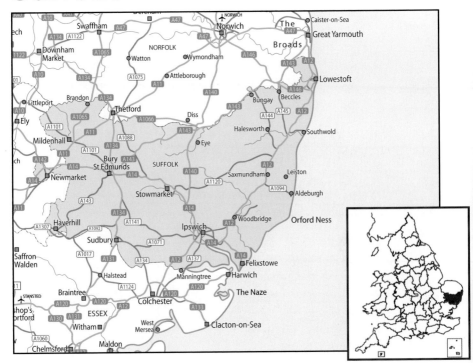

Visit the FHG website

www.holidayguides.com

for details of the wide choice of accommodation

featured in the full range of FHG titles

symbols

⊘ Totally non-smoking	🐕 Pets Welcome
🐎 Children Welcome	**SB** Short Breaks
♿ Suitable for Disabled Guests	♉ Licensed

SB

Badwell Ash Holiday Lodges

A stunning resort of just four holiday lodges positioned around three fishing lakes. Set in five acres in the heart of Mid Suffolk.

As listed in The Sunday Telegraph article "The World's Best Over-Water Resorts

Badwell Ash offers the ultimate year round retreat:
a perfect place for a honeymoon, anniversary or simply somewhere to spend time with friends and family.
Each of the 2 bedroom lodges is graded ★★★★.

- Exclusively for adults.
- Personal outdoor hot tub for each lodge.
- Each lodge with a veranda over the lake.
- All furnished to a high standard with 4-poster beds, fully fitted kitchen and steam showers.
- Complimentary welcome hamper with Champagne, chocolates and many extras.
- All bedding, towels etc included.

An ideal base for exploring the historic market towns and cities, quaint fishing villages, the beautiful coast and many other local attractions that Suffolk has to offer.

BADWELL ASH HOLIDAY LODGES

Badwell Ash, Suffolk IP31 3DJ

Tel: 01359 258444

info@badwellashlodges.co.uk

www.badwellashlodges.co.uk

Bungay, Kessingland, Nayland

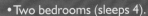

Other specialised holiday guides from **FHG**

PUBS & INNS OF BRITAIN

COUNTRY HOTELS OF BRITAIN

WEEKEND & SHORT BREAKS IN BRITAIN & IRELAND

THE GOLF GUIDE WHERE TO PLAY, WHERE TO STAY

PETS WELCOME!

SELF-CATERING HOLIDAYS IN BRITAIN

BED & BREAKFAST STOPS IN BRITAIN

CARAVAN & CAMPING HOLIDAYS IN BRITAIN

FAMILY BREAKS IN BRITAIN

Published annually: available in all good bookshops or direct from the publisher:

FHG Guides, Abbey Mill Business Centre, Seedhill, Paisley PA1 1TJ

Tel: 0141 887 0428 • Fax: 0141 889 7204

e-mail: admin@fhguides.co.uk • www.holidayguides.com

Derbyshire

SB

Five stone cottages, three sleep four persons, one,
all on the ground floor, sleeps three and one sleeps two.
High and tasteful specification, with exposed beams.
Patio, substantial garden area and wild flower meadows.
The land on which the cottages stand is surrounded by a
nature reserve through which a footpath leads to the River Dove.
* Less than half-a-mile from village and pub.
* Surrounded by footpaths/bridleways and cycle trails.
* Housekeeping standards are of the highest.
* Terms from £240 to £500 per week inclusive.

Telephone: 01298 84447
e-mail: enquiries@cotterillfarm.co.uk
www.cotterillfarm.co.uk

Cotterill Farm
Biggin by Hartington, Buxton SK17 0DJ

Wolfscote Grange
Farm Cottages
Hartington, Near Buxton,
Derbyshire SK17 0AX
Tel & Fax: 01298 84342

Charming cottages nestling beside the beautiful Dove Valley in stunning scenery.

Cruck Cottage is peaceful 'with no neighbours, only sheep' and a cosy 'country living' feel.

Swallows Cottage offers comfort for the traveller and time to relax in beautiful surroundings. It sparkles with olde worlde features, yet has all modern amenities including en suite facilities and spa bathroom.

The farm trail provides walks from your doorstep to the Dales. Open all year. Dogs by arrangement only.

Weekly terms from £180 to £490 (sleeps 4) & £180 to £600 (sleeps 6).

e-mail: wolfscote@btinternet.com
www.wolfscotegrangecottages.co.uk

Please note

All the information in this book is given in good faith in the belief that it is correct.

However, the publishers cannot guarantee the facts given in these pages, neither are they responsible for changes in policy, ownership or terms that may take place after the date of going to press. Readers should always satisfy themselves that the facilities they require are available and that the terms, if quoted, still apply.

Herefordshire

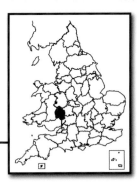

Herefordshire lies on the border with Wales, but is merely a stone's throw from Birmingham, Bristol, the Cotswolds and Cardiff. Green countryside, meandering rivers and acres of traditional cider orchards make up the landscape of this most rural of counties. It is home to the Hereford breed of cattle and has since become recognised for the standard of its local food and drink. Hereford, a traditional Cathedral City but with the feel of a market town, offers visitors an interesting array of shops, cafes and bistros. The Norman Cathedral is home to the world famous Mappa Mundi, the oldest map of the world, and to the largest Chained Library in the world. The five market towns (Bromyard, Kington, Ledbury, Leominster and Ross-on-Wye) all offer something different to delight the visitor, and the 'Black and White Village' Trail explores a group of villages with beautiful half-timbered houses, cottages and country inns. There is something for everyone – tranquil gardens, inviting tea-rooms, castles and historic houses, and of course, plenty of fresh country air.

Lincolnshire

Market Rasen, Skegness

Shropshire

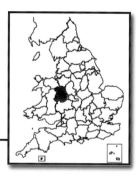

Shropshire is perhaps less well-known than other English counties. This is despite being the birthplace of Charles Darwin, home to the world's first iron bridge (now a World Heritage Site), having not one, but two of the finest medieval towns in England, inspiring the creation of the modern Olympics, and being the kingdom of the real King Arthur. After all, Shropshire is easy enough to find and get to from almost anywhere. (Hint: just north of Birmingham or south of Manchester depending on your direction of travel, and sitting snugly on the Welsh borders).

It may also come as a surprise to find out just how much is on offer. There are plenty of indoor and outdoor attractions, so the weather isn't a problem either. In Ironbridge, you can step into the past at the Ironbridge Gorge Museums where you'll find 10 museums to visit, all following the history of the Industrial Revolution. For retail therapy at its best, small independent shops can be found in all its market towns, full of those special 'somethings' you were looking for and even some things you weren't.

Shrewsbury is the beautiful county town, and home (naturally enough) to the Shrewsbury Summer Season – packed with over 200 events including the Shrewsbury Flower Show and the Cartoon Festival. There is also the Darwin Festival to celebrate the town's most famous son, and the foot-tapping Folk Festival. Ludlow, a medieval town, once the seat of the Welsh parliament, and now famed equally for its events and food, is also full of surprises. The Ludlow Festival is an annual two week gathering of actors, musicians, singers, entertainers, and generally some blooming interesting people to keep you rather amused.

All in all, Shropshire has a surprising amount to offer. So take the Shropshire option – for a great day out, fresh clean air and no jams (except those the W.I. make!)

Visit the FHG website
www.holidayguides.com
for details of the wide choice of accommodation
featured in the full range of FHG titles

Craven Arms, Ludlow

Horseshoe Cottage, Clun Valley

Private self-catering cottage situated in the beautiful gardens of a 17th century Listed house in Clunbury, a village of archaeological interest in a designated Area of Outstanding Natural Beauty – A.E. Housman countryside. Completely furnished and equipped; suitable for elderly and disabled persons.

The Welsh Border countryside is rich in medieval history, unspoilt villages and natural beauty. Enjoy walking on the Long Mynd and Offa's Dyke, or explore Ludlow and Ironbridge.

Colour TV.

Children and pets welcome;

cot available.

Ample parking.

Terms £145 to £200 per week.

Please write or phone for

further details.

Mrs B. Freeman, Upper House, Clunbury, Craven Arms SY7 0HG
Tel: 01588 660629 • www.horsehoe-cottage.com

Sutton Court Farm

3★ - 4★ SELF CATERING

Little Sutton,
Stanton Lacy, Ludlow
SY8 2AJ
Tel: 01584 861305
Fax: 01584 861441

Jane & Alan Cronin

Sympathetically converted from stone barns, these six cottages offer the ideal centre for exploring South Shropshire and the Marches (Ludlow 5 miles).
They are all furnished with care and attention to detail; well equipped kitchens, central heating (two have wood burning stoves), and stable doors allowing in sunshine and fresh air in fine weather.

Children's play room • Pets in some cottages by arrangement.
Cream teas and home-cooked meals can be delivered to your cottage
B&B also available

www.suttoncourtfarm.co.uk   **suttoncourtfarm@hotmail.com**

'A special place to return to'

Staffordshire

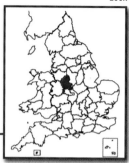

SB

Situated in Staffordshire Moorlands, cosy 3 bedroomed cottage (sleeps 6), overlooking picturesque countryside. Fully equipped, comfortably furnished and carpeted throughout. Cottage, all on ground floor and with three bedrooms (one with four-poster) is suitable for the less able. An ideal base for visits to Alton Towers, the Potteries and Peak District. Patio, play area. Cot and high chair available. Laundry room with auto washer and dryer. Electricity and fresh linen inclusive. Terms from £180 to £350.

EDITH & ALWYN MYCOCK
'ROSEWOOD COTTAGE'
LOWER BERKHAMSYTCH
FARM, BOTTOM HOUSE,
NEAR LEEK ST13 7QP
Tel & Fax: 01538 308213
www.rosewoodcottage.co.uk

Please note

All the information in this book is given in good faith in the belief that it is correct. However, the publishers cannot guarantee the facts given in these pages, neither are they responsible for changes in policy, ownership or terms that may take place after the date of going to press. Readers should always satisfy themselves that the facilities they require are available and that the terms, if quoted, still apply.

Worcestershire

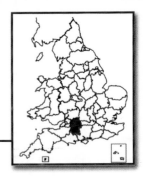

Set in a picturesque 25-acre location in the Teme Valley are our three lodges - *Kingfisher, Woodpecker and Heron* (each sleeps 6). Equipped and furnished to a high standard, with one double, one twin bedroom and bathroom upstairs, and en suite twin bedroom downstairs. Two suitable for wheelchair access.

Attached to the farmhouse is a timber-framed cottage - *Chaff House* (sleeps 2).

In its own grounds, and surrounded by orchards, is *Pitlands Bungalow* (sleeps 6). Two double bedrooms and one twin.

The 3 lodges (ETC ★★★★) have stunning views over the coarse fishing pools (available for guests' use), and the valley beyond. Holistic Therapy by appointment. Outdoor spa. Games/function room - an ideal place to gather when booking multiple properties.

B&B also available in 15thC farmhouse - one twin, one triple en suite and one twin room with bathroom. All with TV and hospitality trays. ETC ★★★★

**Mrs Diane Mann, Pitlands Farm, Clifton-upon-Teme,
Worcester WR6 6DX • Tel: 01886 812220**
e-mail: info@pitlandsfarm.co.uk • www.pitlandsfarm.co.uk

Ratings & Awards

For the first time ever the AA, VisitBritain, VisitScotland, and the Wales Tourist Board will use a single method of assessing and rating serviced accommodation. Irrespective of which organisation inspects an establishment the rating awarded will be the same, using a common set of standards, giving a clear guide of what to expect. The RAC is no longer operating an Hotel inspection and accreditation business.

Accommodation Standards: Star Grading Scheme

Using a scale of 1-5 stars the objective quality ratings give a clear indication of accommodation standard, cleanliness, ambience, hospitality, service and food, This shows the full range of standards suitable for every budget and preference, and allows visitors to distinguish between the quality of accommodation and facilities on offer in different establishments. All types of board and self-catering accommodation are covered, including hotels, B&Bs, holiday parks, campus accommodation, hostels, caravans and camping, and boats.

VisitBritain and the regional tourist boards, enjoyEngland.com, VisitScotland and VisitWales, and the AA have full details of the grading system on their websites

The more stars, the higher level of quality

★★★★★
exceptional quality, with a degree of luxury

★★★★
excellent standard throughout

★★★
very good level of quality and comfort

★★
good quality, well presented and well run

★
acceptable quality; simple, practical, no frills

National Accessible Scheme

If you have particular mobility, visual or hearing needs, look out for the National Accessible Scheme. You can be confident of finding accommodation or attractions that meet your needs by looking for the following symbols.

 Typically suitable for a person with sufficient mobility to climb a flight of steps but would benefit from fixtures and fittings to aid balance

 Typically suitable for a person with restricted walking ability and for those that may need to use a wheelchair some of the time and can negotiate a maximum of three steps

 Typically suitable for a person who depends on the use of a wheelchair and transfers unaided to and from the wheelchair in a seated position. This person may be an independent traveller

 Typically suitable for a person who depends on the use of a wheelchair in a seated position. This person also requires personal or mechanical assistance (eg carer, hoist).

Yorkshire

North Yorkshire

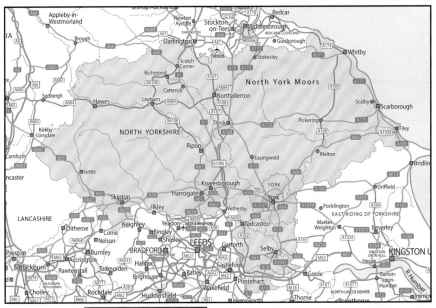

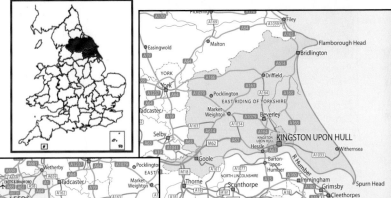

East Yorkshire

South & West Yorkshire

East Yorkshire

Driffield

Raven Hill Holiday Farmhouse

With delightful views overlooking the Yorkshire Wolds, ideally situated for touring the East Coast, Bridlington, Scarborough, Moors and York, this secluded and private four-bedroomed **FARMHOUSE** is set in its own acre of woodland lawns and orchard, with garden furniture, summerhouse and children's play area. Sleeps 2-8+2+ cots. Clean and comfortable and very well equipped including dishwasher, microwave, automatic washing machine and dryer; TV, video and games room. Full central heating. Beds are made up for your arrival; cots and high chair available. Three miles to the nearest village of Kilham with Post Office, general stores, garage and public houses. Available all year. Terms per week from £290 to £640. Brochure on request.

Mrs P. M. Savile, Raven Hill Farm, Kilham, Driffield YO25 4EG • Tel: 01377 267217

symbols

	Totally non-smoking		Pets Welcome
	Children Welcome	**SB**	Short Breaks
	Suitable for Disabled Guests		Licensed

Askrigg, Coverdale, Hardraw

North Yorkshire

Situated in Wensleydale, half-a-mile from Bainbridge and one mile from Askrigg, Coleby Hall is a 17th century gabled farmhouse with stone mullioned windows, the west end being to let. A stone spiral staircase leads to two bedrooms; linen provided. The kitchen is equipped with electric cooker, fridge, crockery, etc., and coal fire. The lounge has an inglenook coal fire and TV. Oil-fired central heating throughout.
Coleby has lovely views and is an ideal situation for walking, fishing and driving round the Yorkshire Dales.

Children and pets welcome.
Terms from £235 to £380 per week.

Mrs E. Scarr, Coleby Hall, Askrigg, Leyburn DL8 3DX
01969 650216 • www.colebyhall.co.uk

Panoramic views, waterfalls, wild birds and tranquillity

Stone farmhouse with panoramic views, high in the Yorkshire Dales National Park (Herriot family's house in 'All Creatures Great and Small' on TV). Three bedrooms (sleeps 6-8), sitting and dining rooms with wood-burning stoves, kitchen, bathroom, WCs. House has electric storage heating, cooker, microwave, fridge, dishwasher, washing machine, colour TV, telephone. Garden, large barn, stables. Access from lane, private parking, no through traffic. Excellent walking from front door, near Wensleydale, Pets welcome. Self-catering from £400 per week.

Allaker in Coverdale,
West Scrafton, Leyburn, North Yorks DL8 4RM
For bookings telephone 020 8567 4862
e-mail: ac@adriancave.com • www.adriancave.com/allaker

Cissy's Cottage

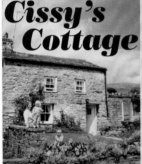

Hardraw, Hawes, North Yorkshire. Sleeps 4

A delightful 18th century cottage of outstanding character. Situated in the village of Hardraw with its spectacular waterfall and Pennine Way. Market town of Hawes one mile. This traditional stone-built cottage retains many original features including beamed ceilings and an open fire. Sleeping four in comfort, it has been furnished and equipped to a high standard using antique pine and Laura Ashley prints. Equipped with dishwasher, microwave and tumble dryer. Outside, a south-facing garden, sun patio with garden furniture, and a large enclosed paddock make it ideal for children. Cot and high chair if required. Open all year. Terms £125-£375 includes coal, electricity, linen and trout fishing. For brochure, contact:
Mrs Belinda Metcalfe, Southolme Farm, Little Smeaton, Northallerton DL6 2HJ • Tel: 01609 881302/881052

Publisher's note

While every effort is made to ensure accuracy, we regret that FHG Guides cannot accept responsibility for errors, misrepresentations or omissions in our entries or any consequences thereof. Prices in particular should be checked.
We will follow up complaints but cannot act as arbiters or agents for either party.

Two well equipped holiday cottages in the award-winning Britain in Bloom village of Darley, between Harrogate and Pateley Bridge. Ideal for touring the Dales, with York within easy driving distance; riverside walks, local pub one mile. Bus stop for Harrogate and Pateley Bridge 200 yards from cottage. Rose Cottage has two bedrooms, one double, one single, open plan lounge with kitchen and dining area. Daffodil Cottage is newly extended and refurbished with a new kitchen with dining area and large lounge. Three bedrooms, one en suite with bath, double and single bed. Further double bedroom and single room, shower room with basin and toilet. Large lawn area. Ample parking. Well behaved pets welcome.

www.southfieldcottages.co.uk

Southfield Farm Holiday Cottages
Darley, Harrogate HG3 2PR • 01423 780258
e-mail: info@southfieldcottages.co.uk

Mile House Farm Country Cottages

Superior Self Catering Holiday Accommodation in Wensleydale, in the beautiful Yorkshire Dales.

**Clematis Cottage • Shepherd's Cottage
Well Cottage • Fell View Cottage**

Traditional old stone cottages of character, recently renovated to the highest standard, yet retaining many original features such as exposed beams and open fireplaces.
Peacefully situated with spectacular views.
Each cottage has colour TV/video, dishwasher, washing machine/tumble dryer, fridge/freezer, microwave, cooker and Aga or Rayburn stove.
Oil-fired central heating, open coal fires • Cot, high chair • Garden furniture • Payphone

**Mile House Farm Country Cottages, Hawes in Wensleydale, North Yorkshire DL8 3PT
Tel/Fax: 01969 667481 • e-mail: milehousefarm@hotmail.com • www.wensleydale.uk.com**

VALLEY VIEW FARM

**Old Byland, Helmsley, York, North Yorkshire Y062 5LG
Telephone: 01439 798221   ETC ★★★★ SELF-CATERING**

Our six cottages, sleeping 2-10 are situated on a working farm within the scenic countryside of the North Yorkshire Moors National Park, close to Rievaulx Abbey and five miles from the delightful market town of Helmsley. There is good walking with several walks mapped into the surrounding countryside from the farm. Enjoy rural peace and tranquillity in an ideal location for exploring Yorkshire. £257-£650 per week. Dogs welcome by arrangement. Choice of cottages for 2. Short breaks are offered, subject to availability. Optional on-line booking.

e-mail: sally@valleyviewfarm.com
www.valleyviewfarm.com

Looking for holiday accommodation?

for details of hundreds of properties
throughout the UK visit:

www.holidayguides.com

Kirkbymoorside, Low Bentham

ABBEY HOLIDAY COTTAGES
Middlesmoor, Near Pateley Bridge HG3 5ST

Commanding unrivalled panoramic views of Nidderdale, and offering peace and tranquillity in an Area of Outstanding Natural Beauty. The cottages are an excellent base for walking, birdwatching and exploring the Dales, Brimham Rocks, Fountains Abbey, Stump Cross Caverns, Masham, Leyburn, Ripon, Harrogate, York and the North York Moors. Our traditional stone-built cottages have been modernised, refurbished and maintained to a high standard. The cottages sleep up to 6 people, and all have oil-fired central heating. All fuel, power, bed linen and towels provided; cot and high chair available. Off-road parking.

12 Panorama Close, Pateley Bridge,
Harrogate HG3 5NY
01423 712062
info@abbeyholidaycottages.com

www.abbeyholidaycottages.com

SB

Hill House Farm Cottages
Julie & Jim Griffith
Hill House Farm
Little Langton, Northallerton DL7 0PZ
e-mail: info@hillhousefarmcottages.com

These former farm buildings sleeping 2/4 have been converted into 4 well-equipped cottages, retaining original beams. Cosily heated for year-round appeal. Peaceful setting with magnificent views. Centrally located between Dales and Moors with York, Whitby and Scarborough all within easy driving distance. Weekly rates from £190 incl. all linen, towels, heating and electricity. Short Breaks available. Pub food 1.5m, Golf 2m, Shops 3m. Pets welcome.

For a free colour brochure please call 01609 770643 or see our website
www.hillhousefarmcottages.com

SB

Bordering rich meadows where sheep and cows graze, our nine highly individual cottages provide a perfect base for those seeking a countryside setting whilst only a short stroll to the lovely old market town. With traditional stone fireplaces, beamed ceilings and delightful pan tile roofs these character cottages are superbly equipped, spacious and tastefully furnished with the emphasis on comfort and relaxation. Nearby are the York Moors & Coast and many attractions including stately homes & theme parks.

Keld Head Farm Cottages

Cottages sleep 2 to 8 +cot
Six of the cottages are single
storey easy access
Price range from
£200 to £1038 depending
on cottage & season
Off peak discounts for couples
& senior citizens

Keld Head Farm Cottages
Keld Head, Pickering, North Yorkshire. YO18 8LL.
Tel. 01751 473974
See our website for VIRTUAL TOURS and all facility details
www.keldheadcottages.com
e-mail: julian@keldheadcottages.com

Luxuriously converted, comfortable and peaceful 18th century limestone farm buildings, centrally heated and beautifully furnished. Well equipped and maintained, most have log fires and are set in mature gardens. All cottages feature fully fitted kitchen, colour TV, Freeview, video, CD player, DVD player, radio etc. Prices include heating, electricity and logs, full linen, towels and cancellation insurance. Pets are welcome at some cottages. Enclosed playground for younger children. Ample parking. Disabled facilities in Hungate Garden Cottage. A short walk from the centre of Pickering, and close to the Moors, York and the Heritage Coast.

Rates from £382 to £1759 per week.

Pickering , North Yorkshire YO18 7ET

Telephone: 01751 476382 • mobile: 0787 6404152

e-mail: holidays@hungatecottages.co.uk

www.hungatecottages.co.uk

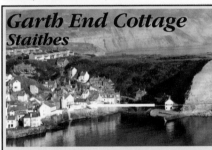

York

Mere Park House · Fridaythorpe, near York

Lovely new house overlooking village green and duck pond.
Situated by the famous Wolds Way Walk. 4 bedrooms.
2 double en suite. 1 single, 1 twin. Large lounge, open fire, TV,
DVD, Dining room. Fully equipped kitchen.
Utility room/washer/dryer. Cloakroom, washbasin, WC.
Oil central heating. Private sunny garden. Parking.
York, East Coast, moors, Castle Howard within 30 minutes.
No Smoking. No Pets.

Contact: Mr & Mrs N. Lazenby
Rossmoor Park Farm, Melbourne, York YO42 4SZ
Tel: 01759 318410

West Yorkshire

Keighley

CURRER LAITHE FARM

Moss Carr Road, Long Lee, Keighley BD21 4SL

Tel: 01535 604387 www.currerlaithe.co.uk

Pennine hill farm rearing 160 cattle, goats, donkeys. The 16th century house and land, covenanted to the National Trust, have panoramic views of Airedale. Desirable six-bedroomed accommodation all year, bed spaces for 15+ people. En suite or private facilities available. Spacious sittingroom, open fire, beamed and mullioned diningroom, inglenook fireplace, seats 20. Fully furnished kitchen. Holidays for families and groups of friends, weekend anniversaries, reunions, mid-week business, social, educational activities. Potential unlimited. 10 car parking spaces. *Terms £100 per day, £550 per week high season.*
Also twin two-bedroomed cottages sleeping five to seven people with kitchen, sittingroom, toilet/shower *from £100 low season, £260 high season.* B&B also available at £20. Pets and children welcome.

Durham

Middleton-in-Teesdale

Self Catering Holiday Cottage • Forest-in-Teesdale

Laneside, a luxury cottage for up to 6 persons, situated in the Area of Outstanding Natural Beauty in Upper Teesdale, is a haven of tranquillity, combining the best features of traditional Dales life with modern facilities.

This former farmhouse occupies an elevated position and enjoys breathtaking south-facing panoramic views of the Upper Raby Estate. It is situated on a carpet of ancient meadows with botanical species and supporting an array of wildlife.

Prices from £290.00 per week.

For further details please contact:

Raby Estates Office, Staindrop, Co Durham DL2 3NF
Tel: 01833 660207 • e- mail: lynda.currie@rabycastle.com
www.rabycastle.com

Looking for Holiday Accommodation?

for details of hundreds of properties throughout the UK, visit our website

www.holidayguides.com

Northumberland

Point Cottages, Bamburgh

A cluster of cottages in a superb location at the end of the Wynding, next to a beautiful golf course on the edge of Bamburgh, only a short drive away from many other attractive Links courses. Bamburgh is an unspoilt coastal village dominated by a magnificent castle and is an ideal base for visiting other parts of historic Northumbria. The cottages overlook the sea with fine views of the Farne Islands and Lindisfarne. Sandy beaches nearby. They share a large garden with lawns and a total of ten car parking spaces are provided (two per cottage). The cottages are in excellent order, have open fire or woodburning stove and are comfortably furnished. Each cottage has its own special atmosphere but all are warm, cosy and well-equipped.

Terms from £205 to £680, weekend breaks from £180. For further information, availability, prices and booking please contact:

**John and Elizabeth Sanderson, 30 The Oval, Benton,
Newcastle-upon-Tyne NE12 9PP
0191-266 2800 or 01665 720246 (weekends) • Fax: 0191-215 1630
e-mail: info@bamburgh-cottages.co.uk • www.bamburgh-cottages.co.uk**

• Etive Cottage •
Warenford, Near Belford NE70 7HZ

Etive is a lovely two-bedroomed stone cottage with double glazing and central heating. Situated on the outskirts of the hamlet of Warenford with sweeping views over open countryside to the Bamburgh coast.

Accommodation is on one level, the lounge is comfortably furnished including a TV/DVD and music centre, fully equipped new kitchen/dining room, one twin and one double bedroom with wash basin and shaver point, bathroom with bath and shower.

•All linen, towels and electricity included.

•Fenced garden with secure courtyard parking.

•Dogs and well behaved owners welcome.

For brochure contact Jan Thompson. Regional Winner - Winalot 'Best Place to Stay' 2004

Tel/Fax: 01668 213233 • e-mail: janet.thompson1@homecall.co.uk

Two spacious stone-built cottages sleeping 4-6.
Recently converted and modernised to give you every facility you require.
Located in the heart of Northumberland on a very tidy working farm with private gardens.
Bolam Lake two miles, Belsay Castle four miles, coast 20 minutes, Hadrian's Wall 30 minutes,
to name only a few attractions.
All linen, heating, electricity included in price.
Sorry, no pets. All children welcome. Brochure on request. Terms £240 to £430.

Mr & Mrs A.P. Coatsworth
Gallowhill Farm
Whalton, Morpeth NE61 3TX
Tel: 01661 881241
www.gallowhillfarm.co.uk

Burradon Farm
Cottages & Houses
Cramlington,
Northumberland NE23 7ND

Tel: (0191) 268 3203

e-mail: judy@burradonfarm.co.uk
www.burradonfarm.co.uk

Luxury self-catering cottages and houses, ideally suited to either holidaymakers or the business person. Conveniently located a few miles from the spectacular Northumbrian coastline and with easy access to Newcastle-upon-Tyne.

Spacious, stylish, self-contained properties with fully equipped kitchens, individually designed sitting rooms, and fully fitted bathrooms with shower. Double glazing, gas central heating and security system. Sleep 2/4/5/8. All towels and linen provided.

A quiet, tranquil setting with good parking facilities and well tended gardens.
One dog per family at extra charge.

symbols

	Totally non-smoking		Pets Welcome
	Children Welcome	**SB**	Short Breaks
	Suitable for Disabled Guests		Licensed

Cheshire

Cheshire - soak in the atmosphere of the historic city of Chester, created by an abundance of black-and-white buildings set in a circuit of glorious city walls, the most complete in the country. Chester's crowning glory is the 13th century Rows – two tiers of shops running along the main streets, offering a unique and sophisticated shopping experience. A leisurely walk along the finest city walls in Britain will take you past most of the city's delights like the stunning Eastgate Clock and the 1000-year-old Cathedral, a haven of reflective tranquillity in a lively, bustling, cosmopolitan centre. The lush countryside surrounding Chester is peppered with stately homes, award-winning gardens and chic market towns featuring characteristic black-and-white half-timbered buildings. Tatton Park near Knutsford is one of Britain's finest Georgian manors, with acres of parklands and formal gardens, a perfect attraction to enjoy in every season, and the host of the RHS Flower Show in July. Or visit Arley Hall and Gardens near Northwich, with its stunning herbaceous borders and Country Fair and Horse Trials in May. throughout the year.

The Old Byre
Pye Ash Farm, Leek Road, Bosley, Macclesfield

The Old Byre at Pye Ash Farm is particularly well designed to suit two families wishing to spend their holidays together in the countryside.

Set amongst the fields but only half a mile from Bosley Village, with its shop and a choice of two pubs, many walks can be taken from the farm, into the fields and woods. Bosley Minns overlooks the reservoir and forms part of the Gritstone Trail. Alton Towers is 15 miles away. All accommodation is on the ground floor, suitable for the less able visitor. The Cow Shed sleeps six and the Sheep Shed sleeps four, both have well equipped kitchen and shower room; rear porch with washing and drying facilities. Ample parking. **ETC ★★★**.

For further details please contact: Dorothy Gilman, Woodcroft, Tunstall Road, Bosley, Macclesfield SK11 0PB Tel & Fax: 01260 223293 e-mail: dotgilman@hotmail.co.uk

Cumbria

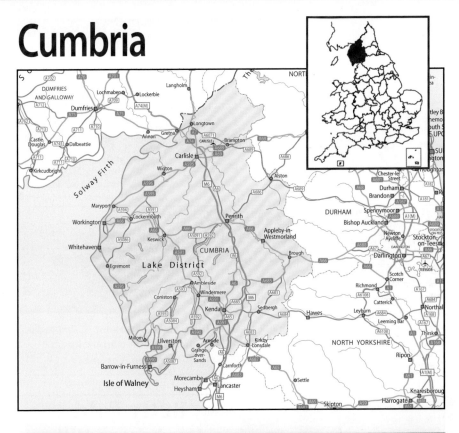

A useful index of towns/counties appears on pages 347-350

lakeland's self catering specialists

Lakelovers

VisitBritain
★★★
to
★★★★★

Quality Holiday Homes in England's Beautiful Lake District

Hundreds of VisitBritain inspected and graded properties throughout the southern and central Lake District. Lakelovers are sure to have a property to meet your needs.
Free Leisure Club membership with every booking

Tel: 015394 88855 • Fax: 015394 88857
e-mail: bookings@lakelovers.co.uk • www.lakelovers.co.uk

Lakelovers, Belmont House, Lake Road,
Bowness-on-Windermere, Cumbria LA23 3BJ

SB

43A Quarry Rigg, Bowness-on-Windermere

Tel & Fax: 0151-228 5799
e-mail: eajay@btinternet.com

Ideally situated in the centre of the village close to the Lake and all amenities, the flat is in a new development, fully self-contained, and furnished and equipped to a high standard for owner's own comfort and use. Lake views, ideal relaxation and touring centre. Close to Beatrix Potter Museum.

Accommodation is for two/three people. Bedroom with twin beds, lounge with TV, video and DVD; convertible settee; separate kitchen with electric cooker, microwave and fridge/freezer; bathroom with bath/shower and WC. Electric heating. Parking for residents.

Rates: Low season £180 to £230; High Season £230-£320

• *Weekends/Short Breaks also available.* • *Sleeps 2/3* • *Sorry, no pets.*

SAE, please, for details to E. Jones, 45 West Oakhill Park, Liverpool, Merseyside L13 4BN

Swallows Nest

Hobkinground Farm, Broughton Mills, Broughton-in-Furness LA20 6AU

Hidden away in the delightful Lickle Valley, some six miles to the south of Coniston and close to lakes and coast.

SB

Swallows Nest is a three-bedroomed cottage sleeping 6-8. Two family bedrooms and third bedroom on the ground floor with en suite and walk-in shower. Spacious lounge with open fire, exposed beams, TV, video and DVD player; dining area; bathroom; well equipped fitted kitchen. Utility room with washer. Oil-fired central heating, ample parking. Sorry no pets. Ten minute walk from our local hostelry which serves good food. From £195 - £895 per week. One bedroom cottage also available.

Contact: Janet 01229 716338
e-mail: enquiries@hobkinground.co.uk   www.hobkinground.co.uk

---

SB

LAKELAND hideaways COTTAGES

Cottages in and around Hawkshead, the prettiest village in the Lake District. Romantic cosy cottages to large houses for that special family gathering.

• open fires • pets welcome • free fishing •

Tel: 015394 42435
www.lakeland-hideaways.co.uk

Hideaways, The Square, Hawkshead LA22 0NZ

Howgill, Keswick

Self-catering cottages in and around Keswick and beautiful Borrowdale

LAKELAND
Cottage Holidays

Lakeland Cottage Holidays provides quality self-catering, holiday accommodation for those visiting Cumbria and The Lake District. Our properties range from quietly situated cottages, through converted barns, apartments and town houses, to larger houses set within their own grounds. Our properties are located throughout The Lake District and Cumbria.

Tel: 017687 76065
info@lakelandcottages.co.uk
www.lakelandcottages.co.uk

Kirkby Lonsdale, Kirkoswald, Lamplugh

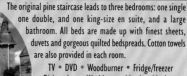

Lancashire

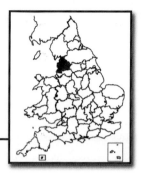

Ratings & Awards

For the first time ever the AA, VisitBritain, VisitScotland, and the Wales Tourist Board will use a single method of assessing and rating serviced accommodation. Irrespective of which organisation inspects an establishment the rating awarded will be the same, using a common set of standards, giving a clear guide of what to expect. The RAC is no longer operating an Hotel inspection and accreditation business.

Accommodation Standards: Star Grading Scheme

Using a scale of 1-5 stars the objective quality ratings give a clear indication of accommodation standard, cleanliness, ambience, hospitality, service and food, This shows the full range of standards suitable for every budget and preference, and allows visitors to distinguish between the quality of accommodation and facilities on offer in different establishments. All types of board and self-catering accommodation are covered, including hotels, B&Bs, holiday parks, campus accommodation, hostels, caravans and camping, and boats.

VisitBritain and the regional tourist boards, enjoyEngland.com, VisitScotland and VisitWales, and the AA have full details of the grading system on their websites

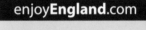

The more stars, the higher level of quality

★★★★★
exceptional quality, with a degree of luxury

★★★★
excellent standard throughout

★★★
very good level of quality and comfort

★★
good quality, well presented and well run

★
acceptable quality; simple, practical, no frills

National Accessible Scheme

If you have particular mobility, visual or hearing needs, look out for the National Accessible Scheme. You can be confident of finding accommodation or attractions that meet your needs by looking for the following symbols.

 Typically suitable for a person with sufficient mobility to climb a flight of steps but would benefit from fixtures and fittings to aid balance

 Typically suitable for a person with restricted walking ability and for those that may need to use a wheelchair some of the time and can negotiate a maximum of three steps

 Typically suitable for a person who depends on the use of a wheelchair and transfers unaided to and from the wheelchair in a seated position. This person may be an independent traveller

 Typically suitable for a person who depends on the use of a wheelchair in a seated position. This person also requires personal or mechanical assistance (eg carer, hoist).

England

Caravan & Camping

Carnevas Farm Holiday Park, Padstow, Cornwall, page 224

Quantock Orchard Caravan Park, Somerset, page 228

Greenhowe Caravan Park, Ambleside, Cumbria, page 225

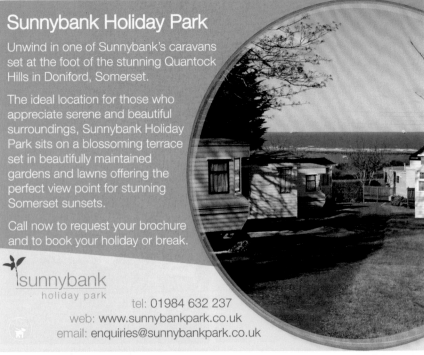

Cornwall

CORNWALL. St Ives Bay Holiday Park, Upton Towans, Hayle TR27 5BH (0800 317713).
The park on the beach. St Ives Bay Holiday Park is set in sand dunes which run down to its own sandy beach. Many units have superb sea views. There is a large indoor pool and 2 clubs with FREE entertainment on the Park.
www.stivesbay.co.uk

SB

Looe

A unique Cornish 4 star holiday experience

Set in 55 acres of rolling countryside well away from the road and with stunning views of Looe Island and the sea beyond Tregoad Park offers the ideal location for both fun filled family holidays and quiet relaxing out of season breaks. Close to the pretty fishing town of Looe and beaches we can guarantee you a beautiful location, all the facilities and a very warm and friendly welcome. We have 190 large flat & terraced pitches of which 60 are hardstanding ideal for touring caravans, motorhomes and tents. Most are southerly facing and all pitches have electric hook-up. There are ample water and waste points around the park and access roads are tarmac so getting on and off your pitch is easy.The toilet and shower facilities are modern, clean and free of charge and there is a launderette and disabled wet room at the upper block. The reception building contains a well stocked shop and visitor information centre together with internet access point and post box.

Tregoad Park, St Martin, Near Looe, Cornwall PL13 1PB • Tel: 01503 262718 Fax: 01503 264777 • e-mail: info@tregoadpark.co.uk • www.tregoadpark.co.uk

Please note

Ambleside, Coniston, Little Asby

Cumbria

A useful index of towns/counties appears on pages 347-350

SB

CAUSEWAY HEAD, SILLOTH-ON-SOLWAY CUMBRIA CA7 4PE

Tanglewood is a family-run park on the fringes of the Lake District National Park. It is tree-sheltered and situated one mile inland from the small port of Silloth on the Solway Firth, with a beautiful view of the Galloway Hills.

Large modern holiday homes are available from March to January, with car parking beside each

home. Fully equipped except for bed linen, with end bedroom, panel heaters in both bedrooms and bathroom, electric lighting, hot and cold water, toilet, shower, gas fire, fridge and colour TV, all of which are included in the tariff. Touring pitches also available with electric hook-ups and water/drainage facilities, etc. Play area. Licensed lounge with adjoining children's play room. Pets welcome free but must be kept under control at all times.

Full colour brochure available.

016973 31253

tanglewoodcaravanpark@hotmail.com

www.tanglewoodcaravanpark.co.uk

M.C. & J.K. Bowman

Devon

The nearest camping and caravan park to the sea, in perfectly secluded beautiful coastal country. Our family-run park, adjoining National Trust land, is only 500 yards from Rockham Beach, yet only five

North Morte Farm Caravan & Camping, Dept. FHG, Mortehoe, Woolacombe EX34 7EG 01271 870381 • www.northmortefarm.co.uk e-mail: info@northmortefarm.co.uk

minutes' walk from the village of Mortehoe with a Post Office, shops, cafes and pubs – one of which has a children's room. Four to six berth holiday caravans for hire and pitches for tents, dormobiles and touring caravans, electric hook-ups available. We have hot showers and flush toilets, laundry room, shop and off-licence; Calor gas and Camping Gaz available; children's play area. Dogs accepted but must be kept on lead. Open April to end September. Brochure available.

Milford-on-Sea

Hampshire

Herefordshire

Leominster

symbols

Totally non-smoking		Pets Welcome
Children Welcome	**SB**	Short Breaks
Suitable for Disabled Guests		Licensed

Hexham

Northumberland

SB

Greencarts is a working farm situated in Roman Wall country, ideally placed for exploring by car, bike or walking. It has magnificent views of the Tyne Valley. Campsite for 30 tents with facilities, and bunk barn with 12 beds, showers and toilet are now open from Easter until the end of October. Prices for campsite are £5 to £10 per tent, plus £1pp. Bunk barn beds from £10. Linen available.
Bed and Breakfast also available from £25 to £40 .
Mr & Mrs D Maughan, Greencarts Farm,
Humshaugh, Hexham NE46 4BW
Tel/Fax: 01434 681320
e-mail: sandra@greencarts.co.uk.

GREENCARTS FARM
www.greencarts.co.uk

Somerset

Taunton

Quantock Orchard Caravan Park

A small, family-run touring caravan and camping park situated in the quiet rural heart of West Somerset. Close to Exmoor and the coast at the foot of the beautiful Quantock Hills, this peaceful park is set in a designated Area of Outstanding Natural Beauty and an ideal touring base for Somerset, Exmoor and the North Devon coast. Personally supervised by the proprietors, Michael and Sara Barrett.
The small, clean, friendly park for touring and camping
Static caravans for hire. B&B available from £18 pppn.

AA

DE LUXE PARK   For colour brochure and tariff call: **01984 618618 or write to: Michael & Sara Barrett, Quantock Orchard Caravan Park, Flaxpool, Crowcombe, Near Taunton, Somerset TA4 4AW**
e-mail: qocp@flaxpool.freeserve.co.uk • www.quantockorchard.co.uk

Visit the FHG website
www.holidayguides.com
for details of the wide choice of accommodation
featured in the full range of FHG titles

Acaster Malbis

North Yorkshire

MOOR END FARM (Est. 1965)
Acaster Malbis, York YO23 2UQ
Tel: 01904 706727

SB

Moor End Farm is a small, family-run caravan and camping site four miles south-west of York. The Tourist Board graded site has 10 touring pitches and six static caravans. Two of the static caravans are available for holiday lets starting from £44 a night or £210 a week.

The hire caravans have colour TV, shower, toilet, fridge, microwave, two bedrooms, kitchen, dining/living area and accommodate up to six persons. Touring facilities available are electric hook-ups, hot showers, toilets, dish-washing sink, fridge/freezer and microwave oven. There are picnic tables around the site for our guests to use.

Moor End Farm is on a bus route to York and is 5 minutes' walk from the popular river bus service and the local inn. We are also very close to the York/Selby cycle track and the York park & ride scheme.

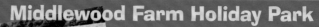

Scotland

Board

Dunclutha Guest House, Leven, Fife, page 245

Glennfinnan House Hotel, Highlands, page 249

Woodwick House, Orkney, page 257

Crosshall Farm, Duns, Berwickshire. page 242

Scotland · Regions

SHETLAND
ISLANDS

WESTERN
ISLES

MORAY

HIGHLAND

ABERDEENSHIRE

14

ANGUS

PERTH AND KINROSS

13

ARGYLL
AND BUTE

STIRLING

FIFE

9

2   6   8

1   11

3   5   7   10   EAST LOTHIAN

4   12

NORTH AYRSHIRE

S. LANARKSHIRE

EAST
AYRSHIRE

SCOTTISH
BORDERS

SOUTH
AYRSHIRE

DUMFRIES
AND GALLOWAY

1.	Inverclyde	8.	Falkirk
2.	West Dunbartonshire	9.	Clackmannanshire
3.	Renfrewshire	10.	West Lothian
4.	East Renfrewshire	11.	City of Edinburgh
5.	City of Glasgow	12.	Midlothian
6.	East Dunbartonshire	13.	Dundee City
7.	North Lanarkshire	14.	Aberdeen City

Aberdeen, Banff & Moray

Attractive, traditional B&B accommodation. Refurbished croft house built in 1899, with modern services. Ideally situated in the heart of Royal Deeside, 30 miles west of Aberdeen off the A93 Aberdeen-Braemar (two miles west of Kincardine O'Neil). Family suite and double/twin room, both en suite, with tea/coffee facilities, refrigerator, hairdryer, clock/radio and power shower.

Terms from £20pppn depending on season and breakfast. Full British, Scottish, Continental or Scandinavian breakfast available • Non-smoking • Wireless internet access available

Mrs Jane Selwyn Bailey, Drumgesk B&B, Newton of Drumgesk, Dess, Aboyne AB34 5BL
Tel: 01339 886203 • Mobile: 07703 203177
e-mail: crogerbailey@aol.com • www.drumgesk.co.uk

GRANT ARMS HOTEL
The Square, Monymusk, Inverurie AB51 7HJ
Tel: 01467 651226 • Fax: 01467 651494
e-mail: grantarmshotel@btconnect.com

SB
Ⴅ
&

This splendid former coaching inn of the 18th century has its own exclusive fishing rights on ten miles of the River Don, so it is hardly surprising that fresh salmon and trout are considered specialities of the restaurant, which is open nightly. Bar food is available at lunchtimes and in the evenings, and a pleasing range of fare caters for all tastes. Double and twin rooms, all with private facilities, accommodate overnight visitors, and some ground floor bedrooms are available, two of which have been specifically designed for wheelchair users. A traditional Scottish welcome and a real interest in the welfare of guests makes a stay here a particular pleasure. *£80pppn, £90 for two people. Bargain weekends available.*

symbols

	Totally non-smoking		Pets Welcome
	Children Welcome	**SB**	Short Breaks
	Suitable for Disabled Guests	Ⴅ	Licensed

Angus & Dundee

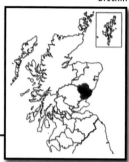

Brathinch is an 18th century farmhouse on a family-run working arable farm, with a large garden, situated off the B966 between Brechin and Edzell.

Rooms have private or en suite bathroom, TV and tea/coffee making facilities. Shooting, fishing, golf, castles, stately homes, wildlife, swimming and other attractions are all located nearby. Easy access to Angus Glens and other country walks. Open all year.

Double £25pppn, twin £26pppn, single £30pn.

We look forward to welcoming you.

Brathinch Farm
By Brechin DD9 7QZ
01356 648292 • Fax: 01356 648003
brathinch@tesco.net

Blibberhill Farm

A warm welcome awaits you from Brian, Wendy and family at Blibberhill Farm, a small, working family farm of approximately 234 acres. The stone-built 18th century farmhouse is situated in peaceful surroundings between the beautiful Angus Glens and the coast. Relax and unwind in our home and beautiful garden. Soak up the sun in our conservatory in summer or relax by the cosy fire in winter in the guest lounge.

Full Scottish breakfast served. Homemade preserves. Traditional Scottish porridge always a favourite. Completely non-smoking house.

All rooms are tastefully decorated and furnished. Clock radios, tea/coffee making facilities, colour TV, electric blankets, drying facilities.

- Spacious family room, with king-size bed and two single beds. Bath, shower, wc and washbasin en suite.
- Double room, with shower, wc and washbasin en suite.
- Twin/double room with zip-link beds, shower, wc and washbasin en suite.

**Wendy Stewart
Blibberhill Farm
By Brechin DD9 6TH
Tel/Fax: 01307 830323
www.blibberhill.co.uk**

---

symbols

⊗ 🐴 🐕 🛈 SB ♿ ⚲

⊗	Totally non-smoking	🐕	Pets Welcome
🐴	Children Welcome	**SB**	Short Breaks
♿	Suitable for Disabled Guests	⚲	Licensed

Argyll & Bute

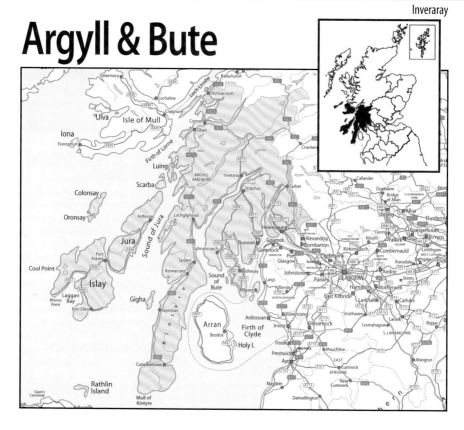

A useful index of towns/counties appears on pages 347-350

Isle of Gigha, Oban

The community-owned Isle of Gigha (Gaelic: God's Island) is known as The Jewel of the Inner Hebrides. The Atlantic's crystal clear waters surround this six-mile long magical isle, and lap gently on to its white sandy beaches - creating an aura of peace and tranquillity.

The Gigha Hotel caters admirably for the discerning holidaymaker with comfortable accommodation and first class cuisine, including fresh local seafood. There are also holiday cottages available.

A must for any visitor is a wander around the famous sub-tropical Achamore Gardens, where palm trees and many other exotic plants flourish in Gigha's mild climatic conditions.

The Isle of Gigha Heritage Trust retails quality island-related craft products, some of which have utilised the Trust's own tartan.

Other activities on offer include organised walks, bird watching, sea fishing, a nine-hole golf course and alternative therapies.

Call us on 01583 505254 • Fax: 01583 505244
www.gigha.org.uk

Palace Hotel

GEORGE STREET, OBAN, ARGYLL PA34 5SB
Tel: 01631 562294 • Fax: 01631 562863
www.rentalsystems.com/book/glenavon

A small family hotel offering personal supervision situated on Oban's sea front with wonderful views over the Bay, to the Mull Hills beyond. All rooms en suite, with colour TV, tea/coffee making facilities, non-smoking. The Palace is an ideal base for a real Highland holiday. By boat you can visit the islands of Kerrera, Coll, Tiree, Lismore, Mull and Iona, and by road Glencoe, Ben Nevis and Inveraray. Fishing, golf, horse riding, sailing, tennis and bowls all nearby. Children and pets welcome. Reductions for children. Please write or telephone for brochure. Competitive rates.

Discounted rates if quoting Farm Holiday Guide at time of booking

SB

Willowburn

Just half a mile after you cross the Atlantic Ocean over the Clachan Bridge you will find the Willowburn Hotel, a small hotel privately owned and run by Jan and Chris Wolfe. Standing in one and a half acres of garden leading down to the quiet waters of Clachan Sound, the Willowburn offers peace and quiet, good food, fine wines and comfortable homely rooms - all in an informal and friendly atmosphere.

www.willowburn.co.uk

Seil Island, by Oban PA34 4TJ   Telephone: 01852 300276   willowburn.hotel@virgin.net

Ayrshire & Arran

symbols

 Totally non-smoking

 Children Welcome

 Suitable for Disabled Guests

 Pets Welcome

SB Short Breaks

 Licensed

Cornhill-on-Tweed, Jedburgh

Borders

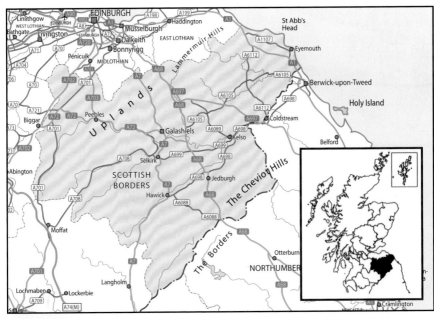

This fine Edwardian farmhouse is situated in the ideal location for visiting the attactions of the "Secret Kingdom" of Northumberland and the wonderful Scottish Borders region. Explore the dramatic coastline with its imposing castles or walk in the rolling hills and valleys - you will find plenty to see and do in this very special area.

Our spacious guest rooms are tastefully decorated and furnished to reflect the period. Comfy seating, period style beds and ample storage. All rooms have colour TV, hairdryer and hospitality tray, en suite or private bathroom. Delicious breakfasts using local produce.

B&B from £35pppn

Hay Farm House, Ford and Etal Estate, Cornhill-on-Tweed TD12 4TR
Tel: 01890 820647
e-mail: tinahayfarm@tiscali.co.uk • www.hayfarm.co.uk

Ferniehirst Mill Lodge

Built in 1980, Ferniehirst Mill Lodge has all the amenities required for your comfort whilst blending with the existing mill buildings and stables. Just south of Jedburgh, situated in a secluded valley, the Lodge is a haven for bird life. Ideal for walking, fishing and horse riding. 8 bedrooms, all with en suite bathroom or shower, and tea/coffee making facilities. Central heating throughout and the spacious lounge has a log fire for chillier evenings. Full cooked breakfast and dinner are served in the attractive pine dining room. The emphasis is on home cooking using local produce. There is a small bar for residents. Personal service and warm hospitality from owners Alan and Christine.

Jedburgh TD8 6PQ
Tel: 01835 863279

ferniehirstmill@aol.com • www.ferniehirstmill.co.uk

AA
★★

Judy Cavers, CROSSHALL FARM,
Greenlaw, Duns, Berwickshire TD10 6UL

A warm welcome awaits you at Crosshall Farm, just off the A697. The house is furnished in traditional style. The bedrooms are decorated to a high standard with a beautiful guest room overlooking the Cheviot Hills. We are in an ideal situation for touring the lovely Border countryside where there is plenty to see, historic market towns, castles, stately homes, walks and lots of golf courses. We are also about 30 minutes from the coast. Bed and Breakfast from £27.50 for twin room with private bathroom and double room en suite. Both rooms have tea/coffee making facilities and TV. After a long and tiring day it's nice to relax in the lounge with a cup of tea and home-made baking.

tel: 01890 840220 • mobile: 07812 801399
e-mail: judycavers@aol.com • www.crosshallfarm.co.uk

SB

This Scottish Bed and Breakfast offers guests a peaceful stay in a comfortable, warm, modern farm house set in 400 acres with cattle, sheep, crops and woodland. Located between Selkirk and St Boswells, just off the A699, in the heart of the Scottish Borders. Our own loch makes a perfect spot for a picnic or swim, and fishing for perch and pike is allowed; grazing for horses. Walkers are close to both the Southern Upland Way and St Cuthberts Way. There are four bedroom suites available, all with private bath/shower room, TV, tea/coffee facilities, etc. Large south-facing garden with patio area, barbecue and furniture. Ample parking. Pets welcome by arrangement. Terms from £22 to £32 pppn depending on season, room and number of nights stay. Packed lunches and evening meals available.

THE GARDEN HOUSE
Whitmuir, Selkirk TD7 4PZ
Tel: 01750 721728
e-mail: whitmuir@btconnect.com
www.whitmuirfarm.co.uk

---

symbols

  SB

Castle Douglas

Dumfries & Galloway

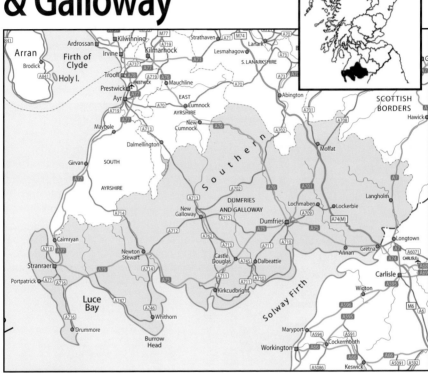

A useful index of towns/counties appears on pages 347-350

Edinburgh & Lothians

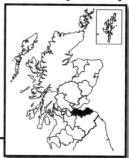

This 17th century farmhouse is situated two miles from M8 Junction 4, which is midway between Glasgow and Edinburgh. This peaceful location overlooks panoramic views of the countryside. All rooms are on the ground floor, ideal for disabled visitors, and have central heating, colour TV and tea/coffee making facilities. We are within easy reach of golf, fishing, cycling (15 mile cycle track runs along back of property).

Scottish
TOURIST BOARD
★★★
B&B

Ample security parking.
Open January to December.
Children and pets by arrangement

Terms from £18 to £25 per person per night, single £25 to £30.

Mrs F. Gibb, Tarrareoch Farm, Station Road, Armadale, Near Bathgate EH48 3BJ
Tel: 01501 730404
nicola@gibb0209.fsnet.co.uk

Edinburgh

Fife

Leven, St Andrews

Kilsyth

Glasgow & District

A working family farm situated close to the town of Kilsyth at the foot of the Kilsyth Hills, a great base to explore central Scotland. Glasgow, Stirling 20 minutes. Croy Station is just five minutes' drive away, where a short train journey will take you into the centre of Edinburgh. Golf, fishing, hill walking and a swimming pool are all within half a mile plus Cumbernauld and Kirkintilloch five minutes away.

One twin/family room, one single room, both with TV and tea/coffee facilities. B&B from £22-£25. Open all

Libby MacGregor, Allanfauld Farm, Kilsyth, Glasgow G65 9DF
Tel & Fax: 01236 822155 • e-mail: allanfauld@hotmail.com

Highlands

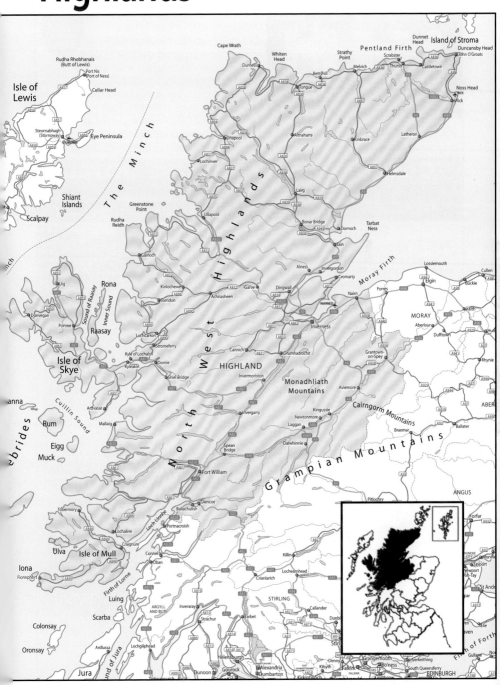

Glenfinnan House Hotel

The North-West of Scotland is rich in history,
legends, myth and magic...
...including the romantic story of Bonnie Prince Charlie

Glenfinnan House Hotel stands just around the bay from the tall monument to him on Loch Shiel, and the famous Glenfinnan viaduct railway bridge is a ten minute walk away through the Glenfinnan Estate, where red deer can often be seen.

The country house hotel is a fine stone mansion dating from 1755, passed down through the family of the original Jacobite owner for many generations, from the time of Culloden.

Today resident managers, Manja and Duncan Gibson, will welcome you into the delightful hall, with its blazing log fire and pine-panelled walls. Attractive public rooms include a Drawing Room and a cheery Bar where traditional music is often played.

The Dining Room offers à la carte dining with a wide choice of speciality signature dishes using local produce.

Charming bedrooms, many with a beautiful loch view, are furnished with terrific old mahogany and oak furniture, huge wardrobes and enormous chests of drawers. Select from a choice of Standard, Superior, Family Room, Family Suite (with adjoining bedrooms) or the Four-Poster Room.
You'll find fresh flowers, fruit and tea and coffee in each room.

The perfect venue for quiet breaks or romantic weekends, in the majestic setting of the historic Scottish Highlands.

Glenfinnan House Hotel
Glenfinnan, By Fort William
Scottish Highlands PH37 4LT
Tel/Fax: 01397 722235
e-mail: availability@glenfinnanhouse.com
www.glenfinnanhouse.com

Lairg Highland Hotel

Lying in the centre of the village, Lairg Highland Hotel is an ideal base from which to tour the North of Scotland. Superb, home-cooked food, using the best local ingredients, is served in the elegant restaurant and in the attractive setting of the lounge bar. All meals can be complemented by a bottle of wine from a comprehensive list. All bedrooms are individual in character, and furnished to a high standard, with en suite facilities, colour TV and tea/coffee hospitality tray. The popular lounge bar, boasting some fine malt whiskies and good draught beers, is just the place to unwind and relax.

Among the many attractions of this scenic area are fishing, boating, sailing and golf, including Royal Dornoch nearby. Local places of interest include the Falls of Shin, Dunrobin Castle and Clynelish Distillery.

**Main Street, Lairg,
Sutherland IV27 4DB
Tel: 01549 402243
Fax: 01549 402593
www.highland-hotel.co.uk
info@highland-hotel.co.uk**

The family-run Northern Sands Hotel is situated on the shores of the beautiful Dunnet Bay Sands, only three miles away from mainland Britain's most northerly point of Dunnet Head. We are conveniently situated for ferries to the Orkney Isles at Gills Bay and Scrabster. The Castle of Mey and John O' Groats are also close by.

The Hotel has 9 comfortable en suite rooms, and public and lounge bars as well as our restaurant, which is known for being one of the finest in the north, featuring finest local produce cooked fresh for you.

The Northern Sands Hotel
Dunnet, Caithness KW14 8XD
Tel: 01847 851270 • Fax: 01847 851626
www.northernsands.co.uk
e-mail: northernsands@btinternet.com

Borgie Lodge Hotel

Skerray, Tongue, Sutherland KW14 7TH

Set in a secluded Highland glen by the stunning River Borgie lies Borgie Lodge, where mouthwatering food, fine wine, roaring log fires and a very warm welcome awaits after a day's fishing, hill walking, pony trekking or walking on the beach.Relax after dinner with a good malt and tales of salmon, trout and deer.

Tel: 01641 521 332
e-mail: info@borgielodgehotel.co.uk
www.borgielodgehotel.co.uk

Biggar

Lanarkshire

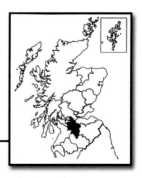

WALSTON MANSION FARMHOUSE

Welcome to Walston Mansion Farmhouse, well known for its real home-from-home atmosphere, where guests return year after year. There is a hearty breakfast menu and delicious evening meals, using home produced meat, eggs, organic vegetables and freshly baked bread. All room have TV/video and tea/coffee making; there is a children's toy cupboard and lots of small animals to see. Pets by arrangement. In lovely walking area and an ideal touring base for the Scottish Borders and Clyde Valley; Edinburgh 24 miles, Glasgow 30 miles.

SB

For details contact: Margaret Kirby, Walston, Carnwath, By Biggar ML11 8NF
Tel: 01899 810338 • Fax: 01899 810334
e-mail: margaret.kirby@walstonmansion.co.uk • www.walstonmansion.co.uk

Perth & Kinross

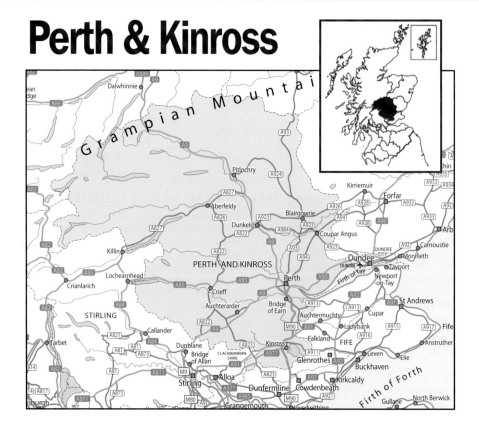

Perth & Kinross embraces both Highland and Lowland. Close to where the two Scotlands meet, a cluster of little resort towns has grown up: Crieff, Comrie, Dunkeld, Aberfeldy, and Pitlochry, set, some say, right in the very centre of Scotland. Perthshire touring is a special delight, as north-south hill roads drop into long loch-filled glens - Loch Rannoch, Loch Tay or Loch Earn, for example. No matter where you base yourself, from Kinross by Loch Leven to the south to Blairgowrie by the berryfields on the edge of Strathmore, you can be sure to find a string of interesting places to visit. If your tastes run to nature wild, rather than tamed in gardens, then Perthshire offers not only the delights of Caledonian pinewoods by Rannoch and the alpine flowers of the Lawers range, but also wildlife spectacle such as nesting ospreys at Loch of the Lowes by Dunkeld. There are viewing facilities by way of hides and telescopes by the lochside. Water is an important element in the Perthshire landscape, and it also plays a part in the activities choice. Angling and sailing are two of the 'mainstream' activities on offer, though if you are looking for a new experience, then canyoning is a Perthshire speciality on offer from a number of activity operators. Enjoy a round of golf on any of Perthshire's 40 courses, including those at Gleneagles by Auchterarder.

The main town of Perth has plenty of shops with High Street names as well as specialist outlets selling everything from Scottish crafts to local pearls. With attractions including an excellent repertory theatre and a great choice of eating places, this is an ideal base to explore the true heartland of Scotland.

Stanley

A family-run farm on the A9, 6 miles north of Perth. Accommodation comprises double and twin en suite rooms and a family room (sleeps 4), with private bathroom. The centrally heated farmhouse has a real coal fire in the lounge. There is a large garden and free secure parking. Situated in the area known as "The Gateway to the Highlands", the farm is ideally placed for those seeking some of the best unspoilt scenery in Western Europe. The numerous castles and historic ruins are testimony to Scotland's turbulent past. There are many famous golf courses and trout rivers in the Perth area, and it is only one hour's drive to both Edinburgh and Glasgow. B&B from £25.

Newmill Farm, Stanley PH1 4PS
Mrs Ann Guthrie • 01738 828281

e-mail: guthrienewmill@sol.co.uk
www.newmillfarm.co.uk

Stirling & The Trossachs

Callander

Riverview House

SB

Leny Road, Callander FK17 8AL
Tel: 01877 330635

Excellent accommodation in the Trossachs area which forms the most beautiful part of Scotland's first National Park. Ideal centre for walking and cycling holidays, with cycle storage available. In the guest house all rooms are en suite, with TV and tea-making. Private parking. Also available self-catering stone cottages, sleep 3 or 4. Sorry, no smoking and no pets. Call Drew or Kathleen Little for details.

e-mail: drew@visitcallander.co.uk
website: www.visitcallander.co.uk

B&B from £27.50 to £30.
Low season and long stay discounts available.
Self-catering cottages from £150 per week
(STB 3 & 4 Stars).

Publisher's note

While every effort is made to ensure accuracy, we regret that FHG Guides cannot accept responsibility for errors, misrepresentations or omissions in our entries or any consequences thereof. Prices in particular should be checked.

We will follow up complaints but cannot act as arbiters or agents for either party.

Scottish Islands

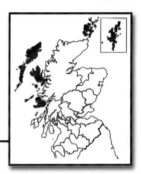

Orkney

Orkney - Less than 10 miles from the Scottish mainland across the Pentland Firth, the 70-odd islands of Orkney are rich in pre-history, but thinly populated in present times. Kirkwall, the capital, is on Mainland, the largest island, where the most accessible and best-known ancient sites are found, inlcuding Maes Howe and Skara Brae. The ruins of Notland Castle on the northern island of Westray, and the famous sheltered harbour of Scapa Flow are other Orkney landmarks.

Woodwick House is a warm, relaxing and welcoming place off the beaten track, an extraordinary, peaceful location set in unique and beautiful surroundings on this sheltered part of Orkney. Run with care and awareness, the house and rooms are simply decorated, tastefully furnished with a homely feel. 8 twin/double bedrooms, some en suite. Two sitting rooms with extensive library, comfy sofas, an open fire and grand views over the gardens; conservatory. Superb cuisine using prime local produce. Non-smoking.

Fully licensed • Packed lunches by arrangement • Drying room • Dogs welcome

Regular events in upstairs concert room including music performances of artists from all over the globe, theatre plays, readings and cabaret.

WOODWICK HOUSE
Evie, Orkney KW17 2PQ Tel: 01856 751330 • Fax: 01856 751383
e-mail: mail@woodwickhouse.co.uk • www.woodwickhouse.co.uk

symbols

 Totally non-smoking   Pets Welcome
 Children Welcome   **SB** Short Breaks
 Suitable for Disabled Guests   Licensed

Looking for Holiday Accommodation?

for details of hundreds of properties throughout the UK, visit our website

www.holidayguides.com

Scotland

Self-Catering

Laighwood Holidays, near Dunkeld, Perthshire, page 285

The Treehouse, Cairngorms, page 279

Kirkton Cottage, Taynuilt, Argyll, page 266

Wilderness Cottages, Loch Ness, page 281

Achiltibuie, Ross-shire, Stac Pollaidh and Cul Beag (photo courtesy of Achnahaird Farm Cottages, page 278)

Appin

Argyll & Bute

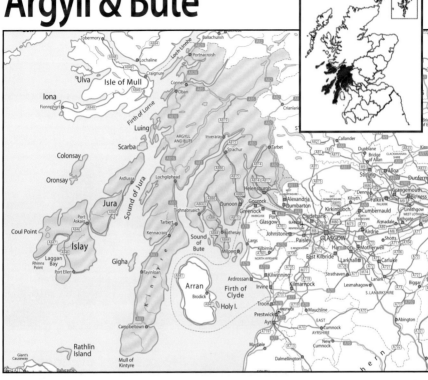

ARDTUR COTTAGES

Two adjacent cottages in secluded surroundings on promontory between Port Appin and Castle Stalker. Ideal for hill walking, climbing, pony trekking, boating and fly-fishing. (Glencoe and Ben Nevis half-hour drive). Tennis court by arrangement. Direct access across the field to sea (Loch Linnhe). First cottage is suitable for up to 8 people in one double and three twin-bedded rooms, large dining/sittingroom/kitchenette and two bathrooms. Second cottage is suitable for 6 people in one double and two twin-bedded rooms, dining/sittingroom/kitchenette and bathroom. Everything provided except linen. Shops one mile; sea 200 yards. Pets allowed. Car essential, parking. Open March/October. Terms from £235 to £395 weekly.

SAE, please for details to Mrs J. Pery, Ardtur, Appin PA38 4DD (01631 730223 or 01626 834172)
e-mail: pery@btinternet.com　　www.selfcatering-appin-scotland.com

SB

Please note

All the information in this book is given in good faith in the belief that it is correct. However, the publishers cannot guarantee the facts given in these pages, neither are they responsible for changes in policy, ownership or terms that may take place after the date of going to press. Readers should always satisfy themselves that the facilities they require are available and that the terms, if quoted, still apply.

SB

Appin Holiday Homes

Appin, Argyll PA38 4BQ • Tel: 01631 730287

e-mail: info@appinholidayhomes.co.uk
www.appinholidayhomes.co.uk

Overlooking sea loch and mountains in a magical setting, our welcoming lodges, house and caravans will help you relax after days of discovery. Families, couples and friends will find a host of activities all close by. Forest, mountain

Full weeks from £205, Short Breaks quote FHG

and island walks, sea life centre, country inn, restaurants, bike hire, garage, garden centre are all within five miles!

And always returning to comfortable accommodation set in 20 acres of maintained land.

Properties sleep up to 6.

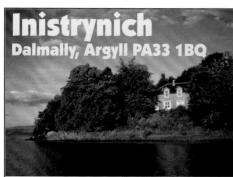

Inistrynich
Dalmally, Argyll PA33 1BQ

Two cottages overlooking Loch Awe surrounded by beautiful scenery, the perfect retreat for a peaceful holiday

- Garden Cottage (sleeps 8)
- Millside Cottage (sleeps 4)

Dalmally 5 miles, Inveraray 11 miles, Oban 28 miles.

Both have garden area, convector heaters in all rooms, open fire in living rooms, electric cooker, fridge, immersion heater, electric kettle, iron, vacuum cleaner, washing machine, colour TV. Cot and high chair by request. Dogs allowed by arrangement. Car essential, ample parking. Ideal for touring mainland and Inner Hebrides. Good restaurants, hill walking, forest walks, fishing, boat hire, pony trekking, National Trust gardens and golf within easy reach.
Open Easter to November.

Colour brochure available, contact: Mr D. Fellowes
Tel: 01838 200256 • Fax: 01838 200253
e-mail: dlfellowes@supanet.com
www.loch-awe.com/inistrynich

Mrs I. Crawford

Blarghour Farm

Loch Awe-side,
by Dalmally,
Argyll PA33 1BW
Tel: 01866 833246
Fax: 01866 833338

SB

At Blarghour Farm, by the shores of lovely Loch Awe, one may choose from four centrally heated and double glazed holiday cottages sleeping from two to six people.

Kitchens are well appointed, lounges tastefully decorated and furnished with payphone, TV and gas fire, beds are made up and towels supplied, while the two larger houses have shower rooms in addition to bathrooms, all with shaver point. The two larger houses are suitable for children and have cots and high chairs. Open all year with Short Breaks welcomed 1st November to end March. Non-smoking. No pets are allowed.

Centrally situated for touring. Illustrated brochure on request.

ASSC

e-mail: blarghour@btconnect.com
www.self-catering-argyll.co.uk

INVERCOE HIGHLAND HOLIDAYS

Invercoe, Glencoe, Argyll PH49 4HP • TEL: 01855 811210 • FAX: 01855 811210
www.invercoe.co.uk • e-mail: holidays@invercoe.co.uk

At Invercoe Highland Holidays we offer you quiet, get-away-from-it-all vacations, in what is one of the most picturesque of the Scottish glens. You can have a relaxing break in a stone cottage, luxury timber lodge, mobile holiday homes or bring your own caravan, tent or tourer for the holiday of your choice. We have been providing holidays for over thirty years and are confident our high standard of accommodation will provide an excellent base to explore the West Highlands.

Self Catering   ★ OPEN ALL YEAR ★

INVERCOE
HIGHLAND HOLIDAYS

Duntrune Castle Holiday Cottages

Five traditional self-catering cottages set in the spacious grounds of 12th century Duntrune Castle, which guards the entrance to Loch Crinan. All have been attractively modernised and accommodate two to five persons.

The estate comprises 5000 acres and five miles of coastline. Without leaving our land, you can enjoy easy or testing walks, sea or river fishing, and watching the abundant wildlife. Nearby are several riding establishments, a bicycle-hire firm, and a number of excellent restaurants.

Prices from £250 to £500 per week. Pets are welcome.

For further details please contact:
Robin Malcolm, Duntrune Castle,
Kilmarlin, Argyll PA31 8QQ
01546 510283 • www.duntrune.com

The Exclusive Highland Estate of

ELLARY

and lovely

CASTLE SWEEN

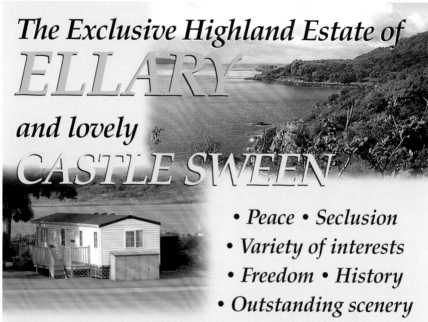

- *Peace* • *Seclusion*
- *Variety of interests*
- *Freedom* • *History*
- *Outstanding scenery*

This 15,000 acre Highland Estate lies in one of the most beautiful and unspoilt areas of Scotland and has a wealth of ancient historical associations within its bounds.

There is St Columba's Cave, one of the first places of Christian Worship in Britain, also Castle Sween, the oldest ruined castle in Scotland, and Kilmory Chapel where there is a fascinating collection of Celtic slabs. There is a wide range of accommodation, from small groups of cottages, many of the traditional stone-built estate type, to modern holiday chalets and super luxury caravans at Castle Sween.

Most of the cottages accommodate up to six, but one will take six/eight.

All units fully equipped except linen. Television reception is included.

Ellary is beautiful at all times of the year and is suitable for windsurfing, fishing, swimming, sailing and the observation of a wide variety of wildlife; there are paths and tracks throughout the estate for the visitor who prefers to explore on foot, and guests will find farmers and estate workers most helpful in their approach.

For further details, brochure and booking forms, please apply to:

ELLARY ESTATE OFFICE, by LOCHGILPHEAD, ARGYLL PA31 8PA

Tel: 01880 770232/770209
or 01546 850223
info@ellary.com
www.ellary.com

Inchmurrin Island
SELF-CATERING HOLIDAYS

Inchmurrin is the largest island on Loch Lomond and offers a unique experience. Three self-catering apartments, sleeping from four to six persons, and a detached cedar clad cottage sleeping eight, are available.

The well appointed apartments overlook the garden, jetties and the loch beyond. Inchmurrin is the ideal base for watersports and is situated on a working farm.

Terms from £407 to £850 per week, £281 TO £560 per half week.

A ferry service is provided for guests, and jetties are available for customers with their own boats. Come and stay and have the freedom to roam and explore anywhere on the island.

e-mail: scotts@inchmurrin-lochlomond.com
www.inchmurrin-lochlomond.com
Inchmurrin Island,
Loch Lomond G63 0JY
Tel: 01389 850245 • Fax: 01389 850513

symbols

 Totally non-smoking

 Children Welcome

 Suitable for Disabled Guests

 Pets Welcome

SB Short Breaks

 Licensed

Ballantrae

Ayrshire & Arran

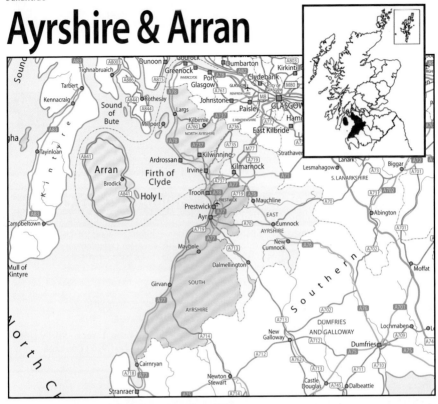

Balnowlart Farm

Ballantrae, Girvan, Ayrshire KA26 0LA
e-mail: marti@ardstinchar.freeserve.co.uk

Tel: 01465 831343

SB

Luxury country lodge situated in lovely Stinchar Valley near old
fishing village of Ballantrae, with shopping facilities, sea fishing,
tennis court, putting green, bowling, golf courses within easy reach.
Beautiful scenery, places of historic interest, many unspoilt beaches,
with rock formations said to be among the oldest in the world.
Ideal spot for touring Burns Country and Alloway, with panoramic
views at Glen Trool in Bonnie Galloway. Daily sailings from
Stranraer and Cairnryan to Northern Ireland. Accommodation for
six comprises sitting/dining room with open fires (fuel included), three bedrooms (two double, one twin), bathroom with
electric shower, fully equipped kitchen, immerser. Heating, metered electricity, telephone. Tastefully furnished throughout.
Linen included. Ample parking – car essential. Pets by arrangement. Available all year. Terms from £150 per week.

A useful index of towns/counties appears at the back of this book

Borders

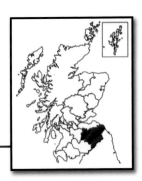

Westwood House – Kelso
Overlooking Scotland's famous River Tweed

TOTAL "OFF LEAD" FREEDOM FOR DOGS IN ENCLOSED AND SECLUDED GROUNDS

Renovated riverside cottage with 12 acres of paths, through walled gardens and on own private island. 4 bedrooms sleeping 2-8 (+ child), 2 bathrooms, period features, cosy log fire and centrally heated. • Half mile Kelso town • One hour Edinburgh/Newcastle • Half hour Berwick (station) and Northumberland coast.

2-person discounts available • Trout fishing also included

ACHIEVING GOLD IN GREEN TOURISM AND 'HIGHLY COMMENDED' IN SCOTTISH THISTLE AWARDS

For brochure and tariff, from £375 per week fully inclusive of all linen and towels, electricity and heating, *contact:*

**Debbie Crawford,
Pippin Heath Farm, Holt,
Norfolk NR25 6SS
Tel: 07788 134 832**

DOGS WELCOME FREE

W
Welcome Host

Edenmouth Holiday Cottages • Near Kelso

SB

Unique, quality cottages, recently converted from a traditional farm steading. Magnificent views across the Tweed Valley. Ideal base for fishermen, golfers, walkers, families and couples wanting a relaxing break. Comfortable, well-equipped cottages on ground level. All bedrooms have en suite facilities. Central heating, linen, towels and electricity included in rates. Large grass garden, games room, laundry/drying room, bicycle lock-up. Pets by arrangement • Open all year
Cottages sleep 1–8 • Parties of up to 18 catered for
Bed and Breakfast also available.

Scottish
TOURIST BOARD
★★★★★
SELF CATERING

Mrs Geraldine O'Driscoll, Edenmouth Farm,
Near Kelso, Scottish Borders TD5 7QB • 01890 830391
e-mail: info@edenmouth.co.uk • www.edenmouth.co.uk

Visit the FHG website
www.holidayguides.com

for details of the wide choice of accommodation

featured in the full range of FHG titles

Castle Douglas

Dumfries & Galloway

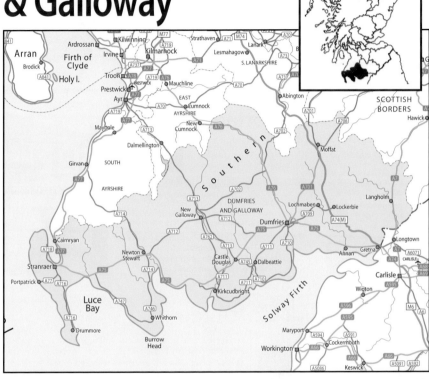

A useful index of towns/counties appears on pages 347-350

Dunbartonshire

The Gardeners Cottages
Arden, Loch Lomond

SB

Secluded in the wooded grounds of Arden House by the shores of Loch Lomond is the row of Gardeners Cottages, built as one side of a magnificent Victorian walled garden.
Linnhe and **Lomond** are ideal for families or friends (sleeping 4 to 5 each), and **Luss** is a perfect hideaway for two. Only 6 miles from the picturesque village of

Luss and world famous Loch Lomond Golf Courses. The cottages are warm, comfortable and full of character, situated amidst breathtaking scenery.

The Gardeners Cottages, Loch Lomond G83 8RD
Tel/Fax 01389 850601
amacleod@gardeners-cottages.com
www.gardeners-cottages.com

The Lorn Mill Cottages
Gartocharn, Loch Lomond
Dunbartonshire G83 8LX

SB

Three contemporary and peaceful cottages set in a traditional 18th century Scottish mill and stunningly located within the National Park. Tucked away in a secluded country estate overlooking Loch Lomond with its tranquil islands and magnificent mountain backdrop, the Lorn Mill provides a unique location whatever the season. The well equipped cottages are perfect for 2 and offer the ideal place to relax, unwind and enjoy unforgettable scenery. Private tennis court available for guests. We look forward to welcoming you.

www.lornmill.com • e-mail: gavmac@globalnet.co.uk
Tel: 44 (0) 1389 753074

symbols

	Totally non-smoking		Pets Welcome
	Children Welcome	**SB**	Short Breaks
	Suitable for Disabled Guests		Licensed

Edinburgh & Lothians

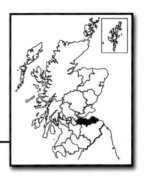

Fife

Fife - whether as 'County', 'Region' or more traditionally 'Kingdom', Fife has always been a prosperous and self-contained part of Scotland. The coast, with small ports such as Crail, Anstruther, Pittenweem, St Monance, Elie and the more commercial Methil, Burntisland and Kirkcaldy, has always been interesting and important. St Andrews with its university, castle, cathedral and golf, is the best known and most visited town. Dunfermline has a historic past with many royal associations and was the birthplace of the philanthropist, Andrew Carnegie. Medieval buildings have been restored by the National Trust in nearby Culross. Cupar, Falkland, Kinross (for Loch Leven), Auchtermuchty and Leuchars are amongst the many other historic sites in Fife, and at North Queensferry is one of Fife's newest and most popular attractions, Deep Sea World. The picturesque seaside village of Aberdour with its own castle is nearby.

SB

East Neuk Cottage

Colinsburgh • Fife

Cottage to let in a conservation village in the attractive East Neuk of Fife, 3 miles from Elie and 11 from St Andrews.
Easy reach of sandy beaches, coastal walks and numerous golf courses.
Two bedrooms, lounge, kitchen/diner and a walled rear garden. Sleeps 4/5, pets welcome. Prices from £275 per week.

For further details,telephone
01788 890942 or see
www.eastneukcottage.co.uk

SB

Stenton Cottage
Elie, Fife

STB ★★★ *SELF-CATERING.*

Terraced cottage situated in the Burgh of Elie in the picturesque East Neuk of Fife. Conveniently located for enjoying large sandy beaches and other amenities such as windsurfing, sailing, sea fishing, golf, tennis, putting and bowling. Several eating places nearby. Along the coast are quaint fishing villages and old harbours and the university town of St Andrews is only 12 miles with its excellent shops, restaurants, golf and golf museum.

The accommodation (sleeps 6) is well equipped with all modern conveniences and has one double, one twin and two single bedrooms, lounge, kitchen/diner, utility room and bathroom; gas-fired central heating. No smoking in the house.

Contact: Mrs J Stirling, 42 Fairies Road, Perth PH1 1LZ
Tel: 01738 442953
www.stentoncottage.com • e-mail: jessie@stentoncottage.com

PITCAIRLIE HOLIDAY APARTMENTS

Luxury Self Catering Holiday Cottages and Apartments near St Andrews in the Kingdom of Fife   SB

Welcome to the Kingdom of Fife

Set within a 120 acre estate of woods, streams, parklands and two ornamental lakes, Pitcairlie is a 16th century castle offering luxury self catering holiday cottage accommodation near St Andrews in Fife.

There are four self catering holiday apartments within the mansion and the original lodge house provides one further holiday cottage.

All of our properties have been newly refurbished to a very high standard, including fully fitted kitchens and gas central heating. Each has been awarded a 4 Star rating by VisitScotland. Our guests are welcome to enjoy our indoor heated swimming pool and sauna.

Besides our holiday apartments and holiday cottage, we now offer Pitcairlie as a very special, historic venue for weddings, corporate events and hospitality.

Perhaps the best facility of all is the peace and quiet of Pitcairlie. Guests can enjoy walking in our secluded 120 acre estate with its woods, streams and lakes. The parklands are grazed by rare-bred sheep and Highland cattle. There is also a children's play area with ponies and a donkey for our guests to befriend.

This lovely rural location is on the Perthshire / Fife border, two miles from Auchtermuchty. Just six miles away is the historic, medieval village of Falkland, home to Falkland Palace, a royal hunting lodge with connections to Mary Queen of Scots. An ideal area for rambling, hillwalking and exploring the East Neuk of Fife, with its sandy beaches and picturesque fishing villages all at hand. For golfers, there are many excellent golf courses within easy reach, including the Old Course in St Andrews and Carnoustie in Tayside.

St Andrews is an ancient university town, famous the world over as the home of golf. From Pitcairlie, the M9 is near at hand, allowing easy access to Edinburgh and the south, as well as north to Perth and the Scottish Highlands.

Scottish TOURIST BOARD
★★★★
SELF CATERING

Pitcairlie House, Auchtermuchty, Fife KY14 6EU
Tel: 01337 827418 • Mobile: 07831 646157
e-mail: reservations@pitcairlie-leisure.co.uk • www.pitcairlie-leisure.co.uk

Highlands

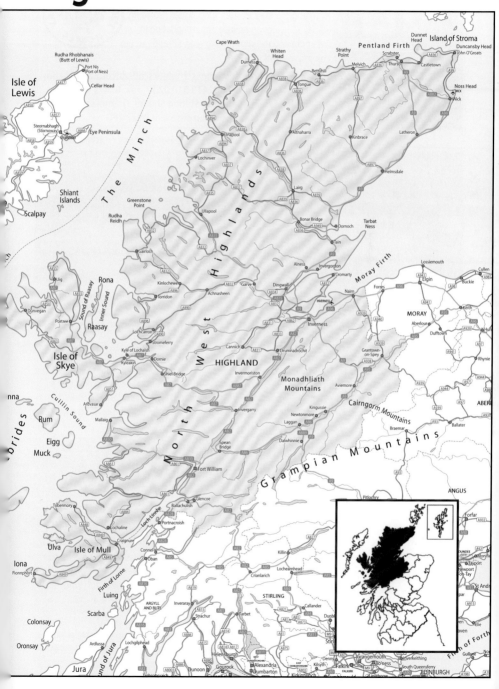

Achiltibuie, Avoch

SB

Achnahaird Farm Cottages
Achiltibuie • Ross-Shire

ACHNAHAIRD FARM COTTAGES are situated right beside a large, sandy beach and sand dunes, with stunning panoramic views across the bay to the mountains beyond. All cottages STB graded 4-star **CUL MOR. CUL BEAG, SUILVEN** and the **FARM COTTAGE,** offer quality accommodation, sleeping 2-5 guests. All have full oil-fired central heating and open fires making these cottages a comfortable retreat at any time of the year. Bed linen and towels are supplied in all cottages Children and well-behaved pets are welcome.

Price range £350 - £515 per week

For further details contact:

Marilyn Mackenzie, Achnahaird, Achiltibuie, Ross-shire, IV26 2YT
Tel : 01854 622348 • e-mail achnahairdfarm@scotnet.co.uk
www.achnahairdfarm.com

SB

Set in the beautiful countryside of Rosehaugh Estate on Ross-shire's Black Isle near the historic fishing village of Avoch, and around 15 miles from Inverness, we are pleased to offer a range of unique, high quality holiday homes. All our properties sleep 4 or 6 people, are spacious, luxuriously furnished and lavishly equipped. The properties are very different from each other, since each one is an historic Estate building which has played its own important role in past times.

The Boat House • Otter Lodge • Red Kite House • Bay Farm Cottages

For details contact Sue Varley, Rosehaugh Estate Office, Avoch IV9 8RF
Tel: 01463 811205 • www.rosehaugh-holidays.co.uk

Tyndrum · Boat of Garten

Completely renovated, well furnished self-catering accommodation retaining the original pine panelling in the lounge.

Set in a rural village, Boat of Garten in beautiful Strathspey, six miles from Aviemore, an ideal base for touring. Fishing is available locally on the River Spey, just two minutes away, with attractive riverside picnic spots. The famous Osprey nest is nearby, at Loch Garten RSPB Reserve. Local steam train journeys, good golf and water sports; skiing at Cairngorm in season. Shop and pub half a mile.

Large lounge, attractive dining/sitting room, spacious fully fitted dining kitchen, shower room. First floor: bathroom, one double and one twin room, both with washbasin, and one single bedroom. Colour TV with Sky digital; dishwasher, microwave, washer/dryer and deep freeze. Electricity, bed linen and towels inclusive. Parking. Large garden.

SB

Contact: Mrs N.C. Clark, Dochlaggie, Boat of Garten PH24 3BU Tel: 01479 831242

Unique lodge in beautiful woodland setting with views over golf course to Cairngorm mountains.

Comfortable, cosy and well equipped with superb log burning fire. Peaceful, yet only minutes' walk from local amenities. Perfect for an active or relaxing break, with wildlife, woodland walks and cycle tracks nearby. Sleeps 7.

*Pets welcome * Weekly lets and short breaks.*

SB

The Treehouse

Phone Anne Mather: 0131 337 7167
e-mail: info@treehouselodge.plus.com
www.treehouselodge.co.uk

Great Glen Holidays
Self Catering - Riding - Fishing

Scottish
TOURIST BOARD
★★
SELF
CATERING

Eight timber chalets situated in woodland with spectacular mountain scenery.
These spacious two bedroom lodges are attractively
furnished with linen provided. On working Highland farm. Riding, fishing and walking on
farm. Ideal for family holidays and an excellent base for touring; four miles from town.
Sleep 4-6. Prices from £250 to £510 per week.

**Great Glen Chalets
Torlundy, Fort William PH33 6SW**
Tel: 01397 703015
Fax 01397 703304
e-mail:info@fortwilliam-chalets.co.uk
www.fortwilliam-chalets.co.uk

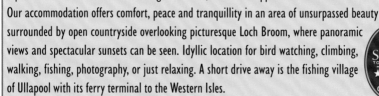

Loch Ness, Spean Bridge

Biggar

Lanarkshire

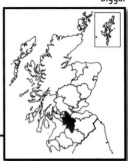

SB

ASSC

CARMICHAEL COUNTRY COTTAGES

Westmains, Carmichael, Biggar ML12 6PG • Tel: 01899 308336 • Fax: 01899 308481

200 year old stone cottages in this 700 year old family estate. We guarantee comfort, warmth and a friendly welcome in an accessible, unique, rural and historic time capsule. We farm deer, cattle and sheep and sell meats and tartan - Carmichael of course. Open all year. Terms from £225 to £595. 15 cottages with a total of 32 bedrooms. Private tennis court and fishing loch, cafe, farm shop and visitor centre

e-mail: chiefcarm@aol.com • www.carmichael.co.uk/cottages

Perth & Kinross

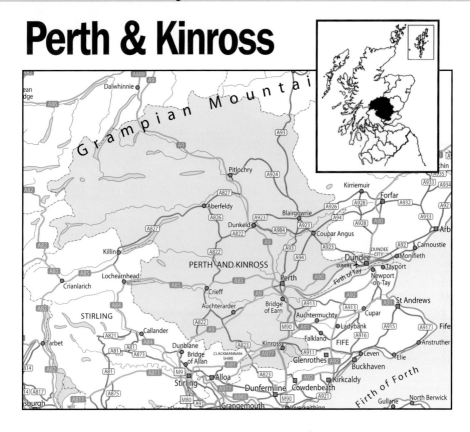

Perth & Kinross embraces both Highland and Lowland. Close to where the two Scotlands meet, a cluster of little resort towns has grown up: Crieff, Comrie, Dunkeld, Aberfeldy, and Pitlochry, set, some say, right in the very centre of Scotland. Perthshire touring is a special delight, as north-south hill roads drop into long loch-filled glens - Loch Rannoch, Loch Tay or Loch Earn, for example. No matter where you base yourself, from Kinross by Loch Leven to the south to Blairgowrie by the berryfields on the edge of Strathmore, you can be sure to find a string of interesting places to visit. If your tastes run to nature wild, rather than tamed in gardens, then Perthshire offers not only the delights of Caledonian pinewoods by Rannoch and the alpine flowers of the Lawers range, but also wildlife spectacle such as nesting ospreys at Loch of the Lowes by Dunkeld. There are viewing facilities by way of hides and telescopes by the lochside. Water is an important element in the Perthshire landscape, and it also plays a part in the activities choice. Angling and sailing are two of the 'mainstream' activities on offer, though if you are looking for a new experience, then canyoning is a Perthshire speciality on offer from a number of activity operators. Enjoy a round of golf on any of Perthshire's 40 courses, including those at Gleneagles by Auchterarder.

The main town of Perth has plenty of shops with High Street names as well as specialist outlets selling everything from Scottish crafts to local pearls. With attractions including an excellent repertory theatre and a great choice of eating places, this is an ideal base to explore the true heartland of Scotland.

Comrie, Dunkeld, Fearnan, Glenfarg

Muirend, South Crieff Road, Comrie, Perthshire PH6 2JA
Telephone: 01764 670 440 • Fax: 01764 670 655
e-mail: enquiries@highlandheatherlodges.co.uk
www.highlandheatherlodges.co.uk

HIGHLAND
HEATHER LODGES

Each lodge
has its own
private outdoor
hot tub

SB

Highland Heather Lodges have been designed for the 21st century with every convenience in mind. The one and two bedroom lodges have open plan living/dining room/kitchens, utility room, wet rooms, and decks in picturesque shared grounds with furniture and gas barbeques. All lodges have full kitchens with dishwashers and microwaves and gas central heating. Auto washer/dryer, colour TV, video/DVD sound system are also supplied. An outdoor timber cabin contains an infra-red sauna. The lodges can be booked separately or linked together with double interconnecting doors to allow one three-bedroom lodge accommodating six in comfort. Bed linen and towels are provided. Wireless internet access

---

LAIGHWOOD HOLIDAYS
NEAR DUNKELD
For your comfort and enjoyment

We can provide properties from a large de luxe house for eight to well-equipped cottages and apartments for two to six, some open all year. All are accessible by tarmac farm roads. Laighwood is centrally located for sightseeing and for all country pursuits, including golf, fishing and squash. Sorry, no pets. Brochure on request from:

Laighwood Holidays, Laighwood, Dunkeld PH8 0HB.

Telephone: 01350 724241 • Fax: 01350 724212
e-mail: holidays@laighwood.co.uk • www.laighwood.co.uk **ASSC**

SB

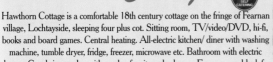

Hawthorn Cottage

Hawthorn Cottage is a comfortable 18th century cottage on the fringe of Fearnan village, Lochtayside, sleeping four plus cot. Sitting room, TV/video/DVD, hi-fi, books and board games. Central heating. All-electric kitchen/ diner with washing machine, tumble dryer, fridge, freezer, microwave etc. Bathroom with electric shower. Good size garden with garden furniture, barbecue. Four-acre paddock for exercising pets, which are welcome. Rates from £240 - £360 per week.

Hawthorn Cottage, Fearnan, Aberfeldy, Perthshire PH15 2PG
For further information please contact:
Fraser MacLean, Clach An Tuirc, Fearnan, by Aberfeldy, Perthshire PH15 2PG
Tel and Fax: 01887 830615 (enquiries are preferred by telephone first)
www.cottageguide.co.uk/hawthorn-cottage

SB

Colliston Cottages

Centrally situated in an ideal touring base for most parts of Scotland, these 3 rural cottages offer lovely views of the Lomond hills beyond Loch Leven. St Andrews and Edinburgh 40 minute drive and easy access to the Trossachs and Stirling. Inverness and even the west coast of Scotland can be enjoyed in a day. Visit Falkland Palace (8 miles) or take a boat trip to Castle Island where Mary Queen of Scots was imprisoned.

Cottages offer comfort and charm and are well equipped, with oil-fired central heating. For a romantic getaway, The Old Cottage, with its open fire and luxurious king-size four-poster bed will not disappoint.

Short breaks available, open all year.
Terms from £220 to £440 fully inclusive.

Contact: Mrs J. Baillie, Colliston, Glenfarg, Perthshire PH2 9PE• 01577 830434
e-mail: colliston_cottages@hotmail.co.uk • www.perthshire-selfcatering.com

Alva, Bonnybridge

Stirling & The Trossachs

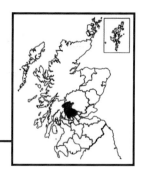

At the heart of Scotland, **STIRLINGSHIRE** has played a central role in most aspects of the nation's life. History and geography have converged here in road and rail routes, in decisive sieges and battles, in important industrial developments and heritage. The county enjoys the natural riches of the Forth valley and the economic wealth of Grangemouth and Falkirk. The town of Stirling itself is a natural tourist centre, both for its own attractions, such as the historic castle and the excellent shopping facilities, and as a base for other visitor attractions close at hand. Villages and small towns such as Drymen, Killearn, Fintry and Kippen offer hospitality and interesting outings. Loch Lomond and The Trossachs National Park is less than an hour from Glasgow, yet feels worlds apart from the bustle of city life. Explore wild glens and sparkling lochs, and for the more energetic, low-level walking, cycling, hill walking, and the new sport of canyoning can be enjoyed.

Scottish Islands

Isle of Islay

A useful index of towns/counties appears on pages 347-350

Carloway

Isle of Lewis

Orkney Islands

Orkney - Less than 10 miles from the Scottish mainland across the Pentland Firth, the 70-odd islands of Orkney are rich in pre-history, but thinly populated in present times. Kirkwall, the capital, is on Mainland, the largest island, where the most accessible and best-known ancient sites are found, inlcuding Maes Howe and Skara Brae. The ruins of Notland Castle on the northern island of Westray, and the famous sheltered harbour of Scapa Flow are other Orkney landmarks.

Dounby

Kebro Farm

A stone built country cottage with spectacular views ...

...and vast peat tracks to walk along, ducks to watch in the mill pond or sit back and relax in the conservatory and just enjoy the view.

This recently converted croft has two double bedrooms, a lounge with kitchenette, and a conservatory. Lovely views of the hills and Scapa Flow. Linen and towels supplied; laundry facilities on complex. Children welcome; cot and high chair available. Pets by arrangement. Just the place to have a peaceful and pleasant holiday.

A friendly welcome is guaranteed

Dr Malhotra,
Greystones, Evie, Orkney KW17 2PQ
Tel: 01856 751283• Fax: 01856 751452
e-mail: vbm75@hotmail.co.uk

LYNNVIEW

5 Star Self Catering Accommodation in Orkney

Lynnview self-catering accommodation is in the perfect location for exploring Orkney, within walking distance of the main transport links around the islands while Kirkwall town centre also has much to offer you during your stay.

Designed to enhance your holiday experience, providing you with an environment built and furnished to an exceptional standard. 3 bedroom house, designed to sleep up to 6 people. Spacious lounge (north facing with views over the town) with wall mounted flat-screen TV (Sky included) and stereo system, fully fitted kitchen boasting top quality appliances, dining area, bathroom with heated towel rail, double bedroom with fitted wardrobes and en-suite facilities and under floor heating. Double bedroom with views over Kirkwall with double bed and fitted wardrobes, bathroom with separate shower cubicle and heated towel rail, twin bedroom with fitted wardrobes. Integral garage, Private parking, utility area and lawn.
All bedding, towels and electricity are provided at no extra charge.

Please contact: Mr Clive Swannie, Lynnview, Holm Road, Kirkwall KW15 1RX
Tel: 07796 498 068 • E-mail: info@lynnviewselfcatering.co.uk • www.lynnviewselfcatering.co.uk

Kinlochleven

Argyll & Bute

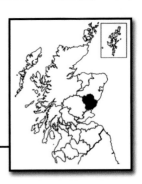

ARGYLL & BUTE is a wonderfully unspoilt area, historically the heartland of Scotland and home to a wealth of fascinating wildlife. Here you may be lucky enough to catch a glimpse of an eagle, a wildcat or an osprey, or even a fine antlered stag. At every step the sea fringed landscape is steeped in history, from prehistoric sculpture at Kilmartin, to the elegant ducal home of the once feared Clan Campbell. There are also reminders of pre-historic times with Bronze Age cup-and-ring engravings, and standing stone circles. On the upper reaches of Loch Caolisport can be found St Columba's Cave, and more recent times are illustrated at the Auchindrain Highland Township south of Inveraray, a friendly little town with plenty to see, including the Jail, Wildlife Park and Maritime Museum.
Bute is the most accessible of the west coast islands, and Rothesay is its main town. Explore the dungeons and grand hall of Rothesay Castle, or visit the fascinating Bute Museum. The town offers a full range of leisure facilities, including a fine swimming pool and superb golf course, and there are vast areas of parkland where youngsters can safely play.

CAOLASNACON
Caravan & Camping Park, Kinlochleven PH50 4RJ

There are 20 static six-berth caravans for holiday hire on this lovely site with breathtaking mountain scenery on the edge of Loch Leven — an ideal touring centre.
Caravans have electric lighting, Calor gas cookers and heaters, toilet, shower, fridge and colour TV. There are two toilet blocks with hot water and showers and laundry facilities. Children are welcome and pets allowed. Open from April to October. Milk, gas, soft drinks available on site; shops three miles. Sea loch fishing, hill walking and boating; boats and rods for hire, fishing tackle for sale.

www.kinlochlevencaravans.com
e-mail: caolasnacon@hotmail.co.uk

For details contact
Mrs Patsy Cameron - 01855 831279

symbols

	Totally non-smoking		Pets Welcome
	Children Welcome	**SB**	Short Breaks
	Suitable for Disabled Guests		Licensed

Dumfries & Galloway

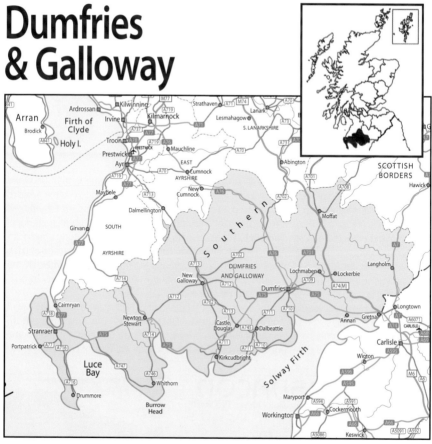

A useful index of towns/counties appears on pages 347-350

Highlands

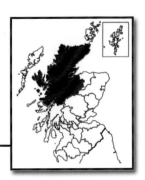

Almost a botanical garden, Linnhe is recognised as one of the best and most beautiful Lochside

parks in Britain. Magnificent gardens contrast with the wild, dramatic scenery of Loch Eil and the mountains beyond. Superb amenities, launderette, shop and bakery, and free fishing on private shoreline with its own jetty all help to give Linnhe its Five Star grading. Linnhe Lochside Holidays is ideally situated for day trips, with Oban, Skye, Mull, Inverness and the Cairngorms all within easy driving distance.

◇ **Holiday Caravans from £240 per week**
◇ **Touring pitches from £16 per night**
◇ **Tent pitches from £12 per night**
◇ **Pets welcome**
◇ **Tourer playground, pet exercise area**
◇ **Motorhome waste and water facilities**
◇ **Recycling on park**
◇ **Colour brochure sent with pleasure.**

Linnhe

LOCHSIDE HOLIDAYS

www.linnhe-lochside-holidays.co.uk/brochure
Tel: 01397 772 376 to check availability

symbols ⊘ 🐕 🐎 SB ♿ 🍷

	Totally non-smoking	🐕	Pets Welcome
	Children Welcome	**SB**	Short Breaks
	Suitable for Disabled Guests		Licensed

Lanarkshire

Perth & Kinross

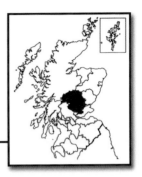

For a peaceful break in the Perthshire countryside, Five Roads is the perfect location. It is situated on the outskirts of Alyth, a small, historic town offering a wide variety of attractions in close proximity. The park is open all year and welcomes tourers and tents. Each pitch has an electric hook-up. There are two Thistle Award holiday homes for hire; each has central heating, double glazing, shower, microwave, TV and is fully furnished. Bed linen is provided. Play area for small children. Pets not permitted in holiday homes. There are three golf courses within a one mile radius.

**FIVE ROADS CARAVAN PARK, Alyth, Blairgowrie PH11 8NB
Tel: 01828 632255**
steven.ewart@openworld.com • www.fiveroads-caravan-park.co.uk

COMRIE West Lodge Caravan Park, Comrie PH6 2LS (01764 670354).

Two to six berth caravans for hire fully equipped with gas cooker, running water, toilet, electric fridge, lighting, colour TV and gas fire. Crockery, cutlery, cooking utensils, blankets and pillows are provided. Sheets and towels can be hired. All caravans have toilets and showers. Pitches available for tents, tourers, motor homes. One modern shower block on site, with showers and hot and cold running water; electric hook-ups; modern launderette and dish washing area, shop. Fishing, golf, tennis, bowling, hill-walking and canoeing all within easy reach. Watersports available on nearby Loch Earn. Ideal for touring, 23 miles north of Stirling and 23 miles west of Perth.

Rates: from £35 to £45 nightly, £230 to £275 weekly; VAT, electricity and gas incl. Tents and tourers £10-£20 nightly.
• Open 1st April to 31st October.
STB ★★★★ *SELF-CATERING*.
www.westlodge.bravehost.com

Please note

All the information in this book is given in good faith in the belief that it is correct.

However, the publishers cannot guarantee the facts given in these pages, neither are

they responsible for changes in policy, ownership or terms that may take place after the

date of going to press. Readers should always satisfy themselves that the facilities they

require are available and that the terms, if quoted, still apply.

Scottish Islands

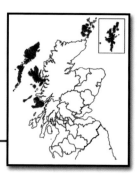

Orkney Islands

Orkney - Less than 10 miles from the Scottish mainland across the Pentland Firth, the 70-odd islands of Orkney are rich in pre-history, but thinly populated in present times. Kirkwall, the capital, is on Mainland, the largest island, where the most accessible and best-known ancient sites are found, inlcuding Maes Howe and Skara Brae. The ruins of Notland Castle on the northern island of Westray, and the famous sheltered harbour of Scapa Flow are other Orkney landmarks.

Other specialised holiday guides from FHG

PUBS & INNS OF BRITAIN

COUNTRY HOTELS OF BRITAIN

WEEKEND & SHORT BREAKS IN BRITAIN & IRELAND

THE GOLF GUIDE WHERE TO PLAY, WHERE TO STAY

PETS WELCOME!

SELF-CATERING HOLIDAYS IN BRITAIN

BED & BREAKFAST STOPS IN BRITAIN

CARAVAN & CAMPING HOLIDAYS IN BRITAIN

FAMILY BREAKS IN BRITAIN

Published annually: available in all good bookshops or direct from the publisher:

FHG Guides, Abbey Mill Business Centre, Seedhill, Paisley PA1 1TJ

Tel: 0141 887 0428 • Fax: 0141 889 7204

e-mail: admin@fhguides.co.uk • www.holidayguides.com

Caravan & Camping
Holidays on Orkney

Looking for Holiday Accommodation?

for details of hundreds of properties throughout the UK, visit our website

www.holidayguides.com

Wales

Board

Egerton Grey, Porthkerry, Vale of Glamorgan page 310

Blaencar Farm, Brecon, Powys, page 307

Drewin Farm, Montgomery, Powys, page 309

The Hand at Llanarmon, Ceiriog Valley, North Wales, page 304

Anglesey & Gwynedd

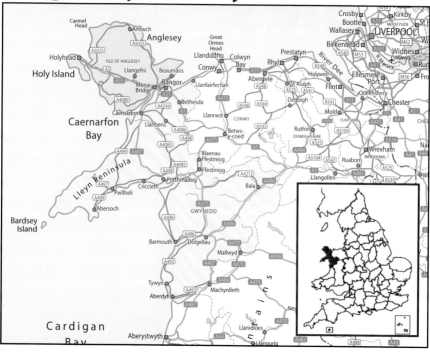

ANGLESEY & GWYNEDD, the northernmost area of Wales, bordered by the Irish sea, has something for everyone. Its beautiful coastline has glorious sandy beaches which offer safe bathing, and there are quaint coastal resorts with attractive harbours and maritime activities, The stunning Snowdonia National Park, right at its centre, covers 823 miles of beautiful, unspoilt countryside and a wide range of leisure activities can be enjoyed. Natural attractions abound throughout the area - mountains, forests, lakes, rivers and waterfalls all wait to be explored, and man-made attractions include castles, railways and industrial archaeology.

symbols

Symbol	Meaning	Symbol	Meaning
	Totally non-smoking		Pets Welcome
	Children Welcome	**SB**	Short Breaks
	Suitable for Disabled Guests		Licensed

Please note

All the information in this book is given in good faith in the belief that it is correct. However, the publishers cannot guarantee the facts given in these pages, neither are they responsible for changes in policy, ownership or terms that may take place after the date of going to press. Readers should always satisfy themselves that the facilities they require are available and that the terms, if quoted, still apply.

Betws-y-Coed

North Wales

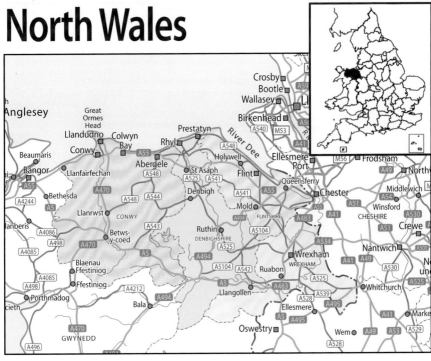

Visit the FHG website

www.holidayguides.com

for details of the wide choice of accommodation

featured in the full range of FHG titles

Fishguard

Pembrokeshire

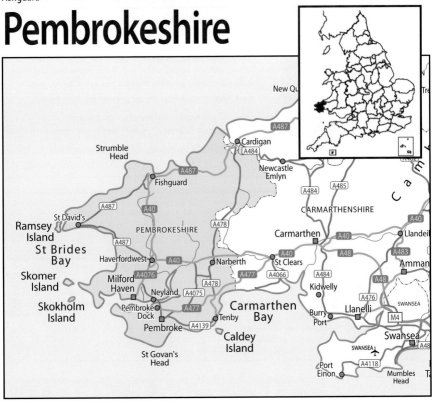

PEMBROKESHIRE'S entire coastline is a designated National Park, with its sheltered coves and wooded estuaries, fine sandy beaches and some of the most dramatic cliffs in Britain. The islands of Skomer, Stokholm and Grasholm are home to thousands of seabirds, and Ramsey Island, as well as being an RSPB Reserve boasts the second largest grey seal colony in Britain. Pembrokeshire's mild climate and the many delightful towns and villages, family attractions and outdoor facilities such as surfing, water skiing, diving, pony trekking and fishing make this a favourite holiday destination.

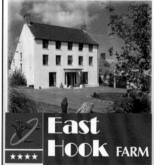

Brecon

Powys

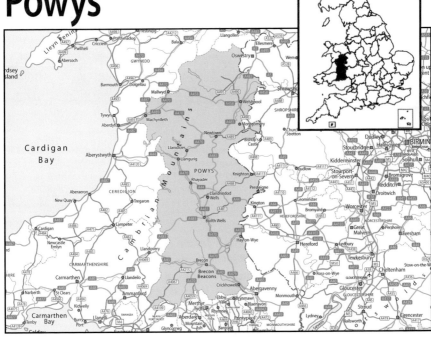

Visit the FHG website

www.holidayguides.com

for details of the wide choice of accommodation

featured in the full range of FHG titles

South Wales

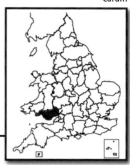

Porthkerry, Vale of Glamorgan,
Near Cardiff CF62 3BZ
Tel: 01446 711666 • Fax: 01446 711690
e-mail: info@egertongrey.co.uk
www.egertongrey.co.uk

Egerton Grey

A recommended centre from which to explore the lovely and uncrowded Gower Peninsula and the Brecon Beacons, this stylish and distinguished country house was opened as a small and luxurious hotel in 1988. Only 10 miles from Cardiff, it is set in a secluded, wooded valley in seven acres of gardens, with views down to Porthkerry Park and the sea. The excellent facilities accorded guests include exquisitely furnished bedrooms (all with private bathrooms), two dining rooms,

library and magnificent Edwardian drawing room. Only a short stroll away is a well-maintained country park with an 18-hole pitch and putt course. The cuisine is outstanding and dining here by candlelight is a memorable experience.

Recommended by many national and international hotel and restaurant guides.

Taste of Wales Cuisine Award

Please note

All the information in this book is given in good faith in the belief that it is correct. However, the publishers cannot guarantee the facts given in these pages, neither are they responsible for changes in policy, ownership or terms that may take place after the date of going to press. Readers should always satisfy themselves that the facilities they require are available and that the terms, if quoted, still apply.

A useful index of towns/counties appears on pages 347-350

Wales

Self-Catering

Secluded cottages in the Conwy Valley, North Wales, page 317

Brynbras Castle, Llanrug, near Carnarfon, Gwynedd, page 314

Trowley Farmhouse, Builth Wells, Powys, page 324

Woodland lodges at Llanteglos Estate, Pembrokeshire, page 320

Anglesey & Gwynedd

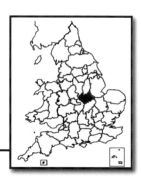

Abersoch

ABERSOCH. Around the magnificent Welsh Coast. Away from the madding crowd. Near safe sandy beaches. A small specialist agency offering privacy, peace and unashamed luxury. First Wales Tourist Board Self Catering Gold Award Winner. Residential standards - Dishwashers, Microwaves, Washing Machines, Central Heating, Log Fires, No Slot Meters. Linen provided. Pets welcome free. All in coastal areas famed for scenery, walks, wild flowers, birds, badgers and foxes. Free colour brochure.

S.C. Rees, "Quality Cottages", Cerbid, Solva, Haverfordwest, Pembrokeshire SA62 6YE (01348 837871). website: www.qualitycottages.co.uk

symbols

⊘	Totally non-smoking	🐕	Pets Welcome
🐴	Children Welcome	SB	Short Breaks
♿	Suitable for Disabled Guests	🍷	Licensed

WTB ★★★

Croeso

SB

• Comfortable three-bedroomed dormer bungalow with enclosed garden • Safe for children and dogs (welcome!) • Near excellent beaches, forest, coastal footpath • Birdwatching area • Snowdonia approximately 30 minutes drive. • Fully equipped; bedding and electricity inclusive • Colour TV/video, microwave • Off-road parking

£230 to £425 per week

MRS J. GUNDRY, FARMYARD LODGE, BODORGAN, ANGLESEY LL62 5LW   •   Tel: 01407 840977

Wales Cymru
★★★★

Plas-Y-Bryn Chalet Park

Bontnewydd,
Near Caernarfon LL54 7YE
Tel: 01286 672811

Our small park is situated two miles from the historic town of Caernarfon.

Set into a walled garden it offers safety, seclusion and beautiful views of Snowdonia. It is ideally positioned for touring the area. Shop and village pub nearby.

A selection of chalets and caravans available at prices from £195 (low season) to £445 (high season) per week for the caravans and £140 (low season) to £580 (high season) per week for the chalets. Well behaved pets always welcome.

e-mail: philplasybryn@aol.com
www.plasybryn.co.uk

Please note

All the information in this book is given in good faith in the belief that it is correct. However, the publishers cannot guarantee the facts given in these pages, neither are they responsible for changes in policy, ownership or terms that may take place after the date of going to press. Readers should always satisfy themselves that the facilities they require are available and that the terms, if quoted, still apply.

SB

BRYNBRAS CASTLE

Grade II* Listed Building

Llanrug, Near Caernarfon, Gwynedd LL55 4RE
Tel & Fax: (01286) 870210
e-mail: holidays@brynbrascastle.co.uk
www.brynbrascastle.co.uk

★★★★

Enchanting Castle Apartments within a romantic Regency Castle of timeless charm, and a much-loved home. (Grade II* Listed Building of Architectural/Historic interest). Centrally situated in gentle Snowdonian foothills for enjoying North Wales' magnificent mountains, beaches, resorts, heritage and history. Many local restaurants and inns nearby. (Details available in our Information Room). A delightfully unique selection for 2-4 persons of fully self-contained, beautifully appointed, spacious, clean and peaceful accommodation, each with its own distinctive, individual character. Generously and graciously enhanced from antiques ... to dishwasher. 32 acres of truly tranquil landscaped gardens, sweeping lawns, woodland walks and panoramic hill-walk overlooking sea, Anglesey and Snowdon. The comfortable, warm and welcoming Castle in serene surroundings is open all year, including for short breaks, offering privacy and relaxation – ideal for couples. Regret children not accepted. Fully inclusive rents, including breakfast cereals etc., and much, much more...

Please contact Mrs Marita Gray-Parry directly any time for a brochure/booking
Self catering Apartments within the Castle
e.g. 2 persons for 2 nights from £195 incl "Romantic Breaks"

Criccieth, Tywyn

CRICCIETH. Around the magnificent Welsh Coast. Away from the madding crowd. Near safe sandy beaches. A small specialist agency offering privacy, peace and unashamed luxury. First Wales Tourist Board Self Catering Gold Award Winner. Residential standards - Dishwashers, Microwaves, Washing Machines, Central Heating, Log Fires, No Slot Meters. Linen provided. Pets welcome free. All in coastal areas famed for scenery, walks, wild flowers, birds, badgers and foxes. Free colour brochure.

S.C. Rees, "Quality Cottages", Cerbid, Solva, Haverfordwest, Pembrokeshire SA62 6YE (01348 837871). SB **website: www.qualitycottages.co.uk**

TYDDYN HEILYN
CHWILOG, CRICCIETH LL53 6SW
Tel: 01766 810441
e-mail: tyddyn.heilyn@tiscali.co.uk

SB

Comfortably renovated Welsh stone cottage with character. Cosy, double-glazed, centrally heated and enjoying mild Gulf Stream climate, with holiday letting anytime. Two bedrooms with sea views. Ramped entrance from outside to an en suite bedroom. Ample parking area and enclosed garden with doggy walk. Positioned on Llyn Peninsula, 3 miles Criccieth, on edge of Snowdonia with a two-mile tree-lined walk to beach.

Conwy

North Wales

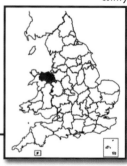

Secluded cottages, log fire and beams
Families will love it – a place of their dreams
Plenty of walks around mountains and lakes
Cosy and tranquil – it's got what it takes.
It's really a perfect holiday let
For up to 2-7 people, plus their pet(s).

Apply: Mrs Williams
Tel: 01724 733990 or 07711 217 448 (week lets only)

Ceredigion

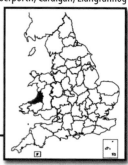

ABERPORTH. Around the magnificent Welsh Coast. Away from the madding crowd. Near safe sandy beaches. A small specialist agency offering privacy, peace and unashamed luxury. First Wales Tourist Board Self Catering Gold Award Winner. Residential standards - Dishwashers, Microwaves, Washing Machines, Central Heating, Log Fires, No Slot Meters. Linen provided. Pets welcome free. All in coastal areas famed for scenery, walks, wild flowers, birds, badgers and foxes. Free colour brochure.

SB **S.C. Rees, "Quality Cottages", Cerbid, Solva, Haverfordwest, Pembrokeshire SA62 6YE (01348 837871).**
website: www.qualitycottages.co.uk

Dolphin Cottage

Penffynnon Holiday Properties

This small cluster of self-contained properties enjoys a unique and special setting in the quiet holiday village of Aberporth on Cardigan Bay. All visitors are delighted when they first arrive and find out just how close they are to the water's edge - every one of our properties is within 200 yards of the sea. It's hard to imagine a more relaxing holiday.

DOLPHIN COTTAGE (pictured) is all on one level (Access Grade 2) and sleeps 6 in three bedrooms. **MORAWEL** has 5 bedrooms and 4 bathrooms, and sleeps 10. **CILGWYN** has been converted into two self-contained villas, each with 3 bedrooms. **TY BROC** is a split level house to sleep 8.

All are very well equipped, and prices include bed linen, heating and lighting. Open all year.

For details contact: **Jann Tucker, Penffynnon, Aberporth, Ceredigion SA43 2DA**
Tel: 01239 810387 • Fax: 01239 811401 • e-mail: jann@aberporth.com • www.aberporth.com

---

CARDIGAN. Around the magnificent Welsh Coast. Away from the madding crowd. Near safe sandy beaches. A small specialist agency offering privacy, peace and unashamed luxury. First Wales Tourist Board Self Catering Gold Award Winner. Residential standards - Dishwashers, Microwaves, Washing Machines, Central Heating, Log Fires, No Slot Meters. Linen provided. Pets welcome free. All in coastal areas famed for scenery, walks, wild flowers, birds, badgers and foxes. Free colour brochure.

SB **S.C. Rees, "Quality Cottages", Cerbid, Solva, Haverfordwest, Pembrokeshire SA62 6YE (01348 837871).**
website: www.qualitycottages.co.uk

LLANGRANNOG. Around the magnificent Welsh Coast. Away from the madding crowd. Near safe sandy beaches. A small specialist agency offering privacy, peace and unashamed luxury. First Wales Tourist Board Self Catering Gold Award Winner. Residential standards - Dishwashers, Microwaves, Washing Machines, Central Heating, Log Fires, No Slot Meters. Linen provided. Pets welcome free. All in coastal areas famed for scenery, walks, wild flowers, birds, badgers and foxes. Free colour brochure.

SB **S.C. Rees, "Quality Cottages", Cerbid, Solva, Haverfordwest, Pembrokeshire SA62 6YE (01348 837871).**
website: www.qualitycottages.co.uk

Terms quoted in this publication may be subject to increase if rises in costs necessitate

Pembrokeshire

New Qu
Tre

A487

Cardigan
A484

Strumble
Head

Newcastle
Emlyn

A487

Fishguard

A484   A485

CARMARTHENSHIRE

A487   A40

St David's

Ramsey
Island

PEMBROKESHIRE

A478

Carmarthen

A40   Llandei

A487

St Brides
Bay

Haverfordwest   A40

Narberth

A40

A48

A483

St Clears

Amman

Skomer
Island

A4076

Milford
Haven

A478

A477   A4066

A484

A48

Neyland   A4075

Kidwelly

A476

Skokholm
Island

Pembroke
Dock

A477

Carmarthen
Bay

Burry
Port

Llanelli

SWANSEA

M4

Pembroke   A4139   Tenby

Caldey
Island

SWANSEA

Swansea

A48

St Govan's
Head

Port
Einon

A4118

Mumbles
Head

PEMBROKESHIRE'S entire coastline is a designated National Park, with its sheltered coves and wooded estuaries, fine sandy beaches and some of the most dramatic cliffs
in Britain. The islands of Skomer, Stokholm and Grasholm are home to thousands of seabirds,
and Ramsey Island, as well as being an RSPB Reserve boasts the second largest grey seal
colony in Britain. Pembrokeshire's mild climate and the many delightful towns and villages,
family attractions and outdoor facilities such as surfing, water skiing, diving, pony trekking
and fishing make this a favourite holiday destination.

Bosherton, Goodwick, Llanteg, Newgale, St Davids

BOSHERTON. Around the magnificent Welsh Coast. Away from the madding crowd. Near safe sandy beaches. A small specialist agency offering privacy, peace and unashamed luxury. First Wales Tourist Board Self Catering Gold Award Winner. Residential standards - Dishwashers, Microwaves, Washing Machines, Central Heating, Log Fires, No Slot Meters. Linen provided. Pets welcome free. All in coastal areas famed for scenery, walks, wild flowers, birds, badgers and foxes. Free colour brochure.

SB S.C. Rees, "Quality Cottages", Cerbid, Solva, Haverfordwest, Pembrokeshire SA62 6YE (01348 837871). website: www.qualitycottages.co.uk

---

Carne Farm

Stone cottage adjoining farmhouse, sleeps six in three bedrooms, also a spacious residential caravan for six with two bedrooms, each with its own garden where children can play safely. In peaceful countryside on 350 acre dairy and sheep farm between Fishguard and Strumble Head, three miles from the sea. Within easy reach of many beaches by car, ideal for walking and bird-watching. No linen supplied. Children welcome. TV, microwave, cots, high chair. Baby sitting available. You can be sure of a warm welcome and visitors can feed calves and watch the milking.

Contact: Mrs Rosemary Johns

Goodwick, Pembrokeshire SA64 0LB

Tel: 01348 891665

LLANTEGLOS ESTATE

WTB
★★★ / ★★★★★

Charming self-contained Woodland Lodges (sleep up to 6) set in quiet countryside estate. Views over National Parkland and Carmarthen Bay from balconies. Ideal for holidays or shorter breaks in any season. Safe children's play area. Elsewhere on the property, visit our wonderful clubhouse - 'The Wanderer's Rest Inn', with fully licensed bar, fire and food. Miles of sandy beaches, many visitor attractions for all ages and rambling trails close by. A warm welcome awaits you. Please telephone for further details and colour brochure.

TONY & JANE BARON, LLANTEGLOS ESTATE, LLANTEG, NEAR AMROTH, PEMBROKESHIRE SA67 8PU • Tel: 01834 831677/831371 e-mail: llanteglosestate@supanet.com • www.llanteglos-estate.com

---

NEWGALE. Around the magnificent Welsh Coast. Away from the madding crowd. Near safe sandy beaches. A small specialist agency offering privacy, peace and unashamed luxury. First Wales Tourist Board Self Catering Gold Award Winner. Residential standards - Dishwashers, Microwaves, Washing Machines, Central Heating, Log Fires, No Slot Meters. Linen provided. Pets welcome free. All in coastal areas famed for scenery, walks, wild flowers, birds, badgers and foxes. Free colour brochure.

SB S.C. Rees, "Quality Cottages", Cerbid, Solva, Haverfordwest, Pembrokeshire SA62 6YE (01348 837871). website: www.qualitycottages.co.uk

---

Porthiddy Farm ❖ HOLIDAY COTTAGES ❖

Near St David's, two attractive stone and slate self-catering cottages with two bedrooms each. Sleeps 4 and 5. Wales' tourist board's 5-star rating confirms the quality and comfort. Set within sight of the sea in Pembrokeshire's National Park, 500 yards from the beach and coast path. Prices include heating, electricity and linen. Pets by arrangement.

Contact Mrs M.Pike, Porthiddy Farm West, Abereiddy, Pembrokeshire, SA62 6DR Tel: 01348 831004 • E-mail: m.pike@porthiddy.com • www.porthiddy.com

St Davids, Solva, Tenby, Whitland

ST DAVIDS. Around the magnificent Welsh Coast. Away from the madding crowd. Near safe sandy beaches. A small specialist agency offering privacy, peace and unashamed luxury. First Wales Tourist Board Self Catering Gold Award Winner. Residential standards - Dishwashers, Microwaves, Washing Machines, Central Heating, Log Fires, No Slot Meters. Linen provided. Pets welcome free. All in coastal areas famed for scenery, walks, wild flowers, birds, badgers and foxes. Free colour brochure.
S.C. Rees, "Quality Cottages", Cerbid, Solva, Haverfordwest, Pembrokeshire SA62 6YE (01348 837871). SB
website: www.qualitycottages.co.uk

Ffynnon Ddofn

Ffynnon Ddofn is situated in a quiet lane between St Davids and Fishguard, with panoramic views over 18 miles of coastline. The cottage is warm, comfortable and very well equipped, with 3 bedrooms sleeping 6 (double, twin and bunks). Attractive lounge/diner with exposed natural stone wall and beams, television, DVD and CD players. Bath/shower room, fitted kitchen and central heating. Washing machine, tumble dryer, freezer. There is a large games room with table tennis and snooker, also a barbecue and pleasant, secure garden. Footpath from lane to beach and coast path. Parking beside cottage. For more information and photographs please visit website:

www.ffynnonddofn.co.uk

For details contact: Mrs B. Rees White, Brickhouse Farm, Burnham Road, Woodham Mortimer, Maldon, Essex CM9 6SR (01245 224611)

SB

SOLVA. Around the magnificent Welsh Coast. Away from the madding crowd. Near safe sandy beaches. A small specialist agency offering privacy, peace and unashamed luxury. First Wales Tourist Board Self Catering Gold Award Winner. Residential standards - Dishwashers, Microwaves, Washing Machines, Central Heating, Log Fires, No Slot Meters. Linen provided. Pets welcome free. All in coastal areas famed for scenery, walks, wild flowers, birds, badgers and foxes. Free colour brochure.
S.C. Rees, "Quality Cottages", Cerbid, Solva, Haverfordwest, Pembrokeshire SA62 6YE (01348 837871). SB
website: www.qualitycottages.co.uk

TENBY. Around the magnificent Welsh Coast. Away from the madding crowd. Near safe sandy beaches. A small specialist agency offering privacy, peace and unashamed luxury. First Wales Tourist Board Self Catering Gold Award Winner. Residential standards - Dishwashers, Microwaves, Washing Machines, Central Heating, Log Fires, No Slot Meters. Linen provided. Pets welcome free. All in coastal areas famed for scenery, walks, wild flowers, birds, badgers and foxes. Free colour brochure.
S.C. Rees, "Quality Cottages", Cerbid, Solva, Haverfordwest, Pembrokeshire SA62 6YE (01348 837871). SB
website: www.qualitycottages.co.uk

A country estate of over 450 acres, including 2 miles of riverbank. See a real farm in action, the hustle and bustle of harvest, newborn calves and lambs. Choose from 6 character stone cottages, lovingly converted traditional farm buildings, some over 200 years old.

www.davidsfarm.com

Each cottage is fully furnished and equipped, electricity and linen included, with all year round heating. Children welcome. Brochure available. Contact: **Mrs Angela Colledge, Gwarmacwydd, Llanfallteg, Whitland, Pembrokeshire SA34 0XH**

Self Catering ★★★★ Cottages   t 0800 321 3699

SB

Powys

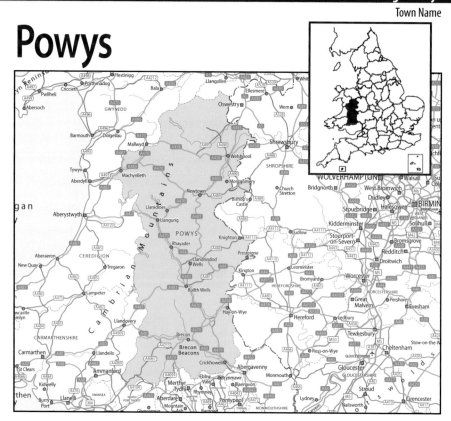

POWYS is situated right on England's doorstep and boasts some of the most spectacular scenery in Europe. Ideal for an action packed holiday with fishing, golfing, pony trekking, sailing and canal cruising readily available, and walkers have a choice of everything from riverside trails to mountain hikes. Offa's Dyke Path and Glyndwr's Way pass through the region. Offa's Dyke Path runs for 177 miles through Border country, often following the ancient earthworks, while Glyndwr's Way takes in some of the finest landscape features in Wales on its journey from Knighton to Machynlleth and back to the borders at Welshpool.

There are border towns with Georgian architecture and half-timbered black and white houses to visit, or wander round the wonderful shops in the book town of Hay, famous for its Literary Festival each May. There are Victorian spa towns too, with even the smallest of places holding festivals and events throughout the year.

A useful index of towns/counties appears on pages 347-350

PENLLWYN LODGES
SELF CATERING HOLIDAYS

A Superb Holiday Setting for all Seasons

Self-catering Log Cabins set in 30 acres of unspoilt woodland teeming with wild life. Fishing on the Montgomery Canal, River Severn, and our own private lake. Quad trekking, pony trekking, castles, and lakes nearby.

Each cabin sleeping 2-8 people has central heating, colour TV, microwave, full kitchen, bath/shower, and includes all bedding. Pets welcome in certain cabins.

From £175 - £692 per cabin per week (including VAT)

Telephone/Fax for colour brochure:

01686 640269

PENLLWYN LODGES
GARTHMYL, POWYS SYI5 6SB

e-mail: daphne.jones@onetel.net
www.penllwynlodges.co.uk

TROWLEY FARMHOUSE. Detached farmhouse in unspoilt location on 400-acre working farm. Views of Black Mountains and Brecon Beacons. Oak beams, stone walls and large farmhouse kitchen retain much of the 16th century character, with every modern convenience to make your stay comfortable.

Sleeps up to 14 • One family bathroom, two en suite bathrooms, one downstairs bathroom/shower room. Two twin rooms and one family room, one double room, one bunk bed room, sleeps 4 • All fuel and linen (except towels) incl. • Home-cooked meal service • Ample parking, garden with barbecue • A warm welcome for you and your pets.

Mr Ben Lewis, LLanbedr Hall, Painscastle, Builth Wells, Powys LD2 3JH
01497 851665 • e-mail: ruth@trowleyfarmhouse.co.uk

www.trowleyfarmhouse.co.uk

WTB ★★★★

SB

Highgate Holiday Cottages are situated 3 miles from Newtown, a charming market town on the Welsh Borders. There are six beautifully appointed, newly converted, luxury self-catering barn cottages, three sleeping 8 and three sleeping 6. Set in a traditional old farmyard setting with trout pool and beautiful gardens.
• All have underfloor heating throughout and are decorated, furnished and equipped to a very high standard • Bed linen and towels provided
• Barbecue and furniture • Ample parking
• 20 acres of private pastureland with woodland and wildlife pool. Quarry Cottage is disabled-friendly.

Contact: Chris & Sarah Smith, Highgate, Near Newtown SY16 3LF
Tel: 01686 623763 • Fax: 01686 629194
e-mail: highgatehouse@hotmail.com
www.highgate-accommodation.co.uk

Short Breaks available

SB

South Wales

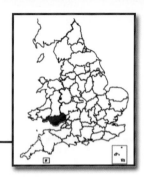

symbols

	Totally non-smoking			Pets Welcome
	Children Welcome		**SB**	Short Breaks
	Suitable for Disabled Guests		♇	Licensed

WALES
Caravans & Camping
Anglesey & Gwynedd

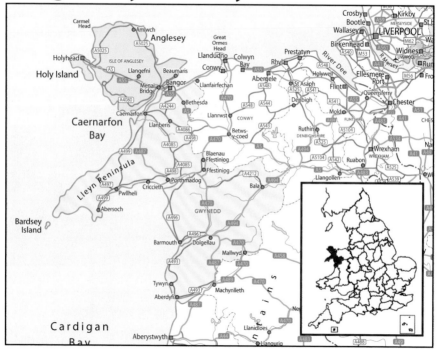

ANGLESEY & GWYNEDD, the northernmost area of Wales, bordered by the Irish sea, has something for everyone. Its beautiful coastline has glorious sandy beaches which offer safe bathing, and there are quaint coastal resorts with attractive harbours and maritime activities, The stunning Snowdonia National Park, right at its centre, covers 823 miles of beautiful, unspoilt countryside and a wide range of leisure activities can be enjoyed. Natural attractions abound throughout the area - mountains, forests, lakes, rivers and waterfalls all wait to be explored, and man-made attractions include castles, railways and industrial archaeology.

A useful index of towns/counties appears at the back of this book

SB

Static six-berth luxury caravan with two bedrooms, shower, bathroom, colour TV, microwave, etc. on private grounds.

Situated two miles from Bala in beautiful country area.

Ideal for walking, sailing,

fishing and canoeing.

30 miles from nearest beach.

Pets welcome.

Contact: **MRS A. SKINNER,**
TY GWYN, RHYDUCHAF,
BALA, GWYNEDD LL23 7SD
Tel: 01678 521267

TYN RHÔS CAMPING SITE Ravenspoint Road,
Trearddur Bay, Holyhead, Isle of Anglesey LL65 2AX • 01407 860369

VisitWales
★★★

SB

Clean facilities, hot showers, toilets, chemical disposal, electric hook-ups etc. Couples and families welcome; separate rally field available; some disabled access - access statement/ further information on request.

Rocky coves and sandy bays, Blue Flag beaches and public slipway, horse riding, golf, spectacular coastal views - all on the doorstep. Discover this diverse island steeped in history with its many attractions. Ferries to Ireland 3 miles.

Access from the A55. Junction 2 for Trearddur Bay
on the B4545, turn right onto Ravenspoint Road,
(after Spar shop), one mile to shared entrance, bear left.

Publisher's note

While every effort is made to ensure accuracy, we regret that FHG Guides cannot accept responsibility for errors, misrepresentations or omissions in our entries or any consequences thereof. Prices in particular should be checked.

We will follow up complaints but cannot act as arbiters or agents for either party.

Ireland
Co. Clare

County Clare

Ballyvaughan Village and Country Holiday Homes

Offering a range of quality self-catering holiday accommodation in the unspoilt and charming village of Ballyvaughan on the southern shores of Galway Bay in the heartland of the world famous Burren district of County Clare. You can choose from our cottages, which sleep up to six, or our apartments, which sleep up to three. All our village accommodation is located in the centre of the village with a good choice of restaurants and pubs. Our location is an ideal base to explore the unique Burren landscape or tour the west coast of Ireland. Open all year and very suitable for off-season bookings.

Visit our comprehensive website for more details. Terms from €299 to €830.

**Mr George Quinn, Main Street, Ballyvaughan, Co.Clare • 00353 87 2428161
e-mail: vchh@iol.ie • www.ballyvaughan-cottages.com**

Other specialised holiday guides from FHG

PUBS & INNS OF BRITAIN • **COUNTRY HOTELS** OF BRITAIN

WEEKEND & SHORT BREAK HOLIDAYS IN BRITAIN

THE GOLF GUIDE WHERE TO PLAY, WHERE TO STAY

500 GREAT PLACES TO STAY • **SELF-CATERING HOLIDAYS** IN BRITAIN

BED & BREAKFAST STOPS • **CARAVAN & CAMPING HOLIDAYS**

FAMILY BREAKS IN BRITAIN

Published annually: available in all good bookshops or direct from the publisher:
FHG Guides, Abbey Mill Business Centre, Seedhill, Paisley PA1 1TJ
Tel: 0141 887 0428 • Fax: 0141 889 7204
e-mail: admin@fhguides.co.uk • www.holidayguides.com

Country Inns

Cornwall

Bodmin Moor

Colliford Tavern   "AN OASIS ON BODMIN MOOR"

Colliford Lake, Near St Neot, Liskeard, Cornwall PL14 6PZ • Tel: 01208 821335
e-mail: info@colliford.com • www.colliford.com

Set in attractive grounds which include a children's play area, ponds and a working waterwheel, this delightfully furnished free house offers good food and bar snacks. Sprucely-appointed guest rooms are spacious and have en suite shower, colour television, radio alarm, beverage maker and numerous thoughtful extras.

An unusual feature of the tavern is a 37' deep granite well. In the midst of the scenic splendour of Bodmin Moor, this is a relaxing country retreat only a few minutes' walk from Colliford Lake, so popular with fly fishermen. Both north and south coasts are within easy driving distance and terms are most reasonable.

★★★
INN

Campsite for touring caravans, motorhomes and tents - full electric hook-up etc available.

SB

Cumbria

Brampton, Coniston

Talkin Village, Brampton, Cumbria CA8 1LE
Tel: 016977 3452 • Fax: 016977 3396
e-mail: blacksmithsarmstalkin@yahoo.co.uk
www.blacksmithstalkin.co.uk
The Blacksmith's Arms offers all the hospitality and comforts of a traditional country inn. Enjoy tasty meals served in the bar lounges, or linger over dinner in the well-appointed restaurant. The inn is personally managed by the proprietors, Anne and Donald Jackson, who guarantee the hospitality one would expect from a family concern. Guests are assured of a pleasant and comfortable stay. There are eight lovely bedrooms, all en suite. Peacefully situated in the beautiful village of Talkin, the inn is convenient for the Borders, Hadrian's Wall and the Lake District. There is a good golf course, walking and other country pursuits nearby.

A superbly located 10-bedroom hotel designed to overlook the village and enjoy panoramic mountain views. With a large private garden, patio, comfortable lounge, and extensive restaurant menu and wine list, the hotel offers comfortable en suite accommodation in a peaceful and informal setting. All bedrooms have been recently refurbished, with a relaxing night's sleep as good as promised! Better still, when built (in 1902), the hotel was attached to the end of a 16th century pub! It is now a freehouse with real ales and real fires in a classic Lakeland setting of beamed ceiling, flagged floor and an old range.

Sun Hotel & 16th Century Inn

Coniston LA21 8HQ • Tel: 015394 41248
Fax: 015394 41219 • info@thesunconiston.com
www.thesunconiston.com

Gloucestershire

Parkend

THE FOUNTAIN INN & LODGE

Parkend, Royal Forest of Dean, Gloucestershire GL15 4JD.

Traditional village inn, well known locally for its excellent meals and real ales. A Forest Fayre menu offers such delicious main courses as Lamb Shank In Redcurrant & Rosemary Sauce and Gloucester Sausage in Onion Gravy, together with a large selection of curries and vegetarian dishes.

Centrally situated in one of England's foremost wooded areas, the inn makes an ideal base for sightseeing, or for exploring some of the many peaceful forest walks nearby.

All bedrooms (including two specially adapted for the less able) are en suite, decorated and furnished to an excellent standard, and have television and tea/coffee making facilities. Various half-board breaks are available throughout the year.

Tel: 01594 562189 • Fax: 01594 564438 • e-mail: thefountaininn@aol.com • www.thefountaininnandlodge.com

Shropshire

Bishop's Castle

The Travellers Rest Inn

**Upper Affcot
Church Stretton SY6 6RL
Tel: 01694 781275
Fax: 01694 781555
reception@travellersrestinn.co.uk
www.travellersrestinn.co.uk**

Situated between Church Stretton and Craven Arms, and surrounded by The South Shropshire Hills. We, Fraser and Mauresia Allison, the owners assure you a warm welcome, good food, good beers, good accommodation, and good old fashioned service.

For those wishing to stay overnight with us at The Travellers Rest we have 12 very nice en suite guest bedrooms: six of these being on the ground floor with easy access, and two of these are suitable for accompanied wheel chair users. The bedrooms are away from the main area of the Inn and have their own entrance to the car park and garden, ideal if you have brought your pet with you and a midnight walk is needed.

Our well stocked Bar can satisfy most thirsts; cask ales, lagers, stouts, spirits, wines and minerals, throughout the day and the Kitchen takes care of your hunger; be it for a snack or a full satisfying meal, vegetarians no problem, food being served until 9pm in the evening.

Publisher's note

symbols

	Totally non-smoking		Pets Welcome
	Children Welcome	**SB**	Short Breaks
	Suitable for Disabled Guests		Licensed

Suffolk

Bury St Edmunds

Please note

All the information in this book is given in good faith in the belief that it is correct. However, the publishers cannot guarantee the facts given in these pages, neither are they responsible for changes in policy, ownership or terms that may take place after the date of going to press. Readers should always satisfy themselves that the facilities they require are available and that the terms, if quoted, still apply.

East Yorkshire

See opposite

THE WOLDS INN
Driffield Road, Huggate,
East Yorkshire YO42 IYH
Tel: 01377 288217
huggate@woldsinn.freeserve.co.uk

A peaceful country inn in farming country high in the Wolds,
the hostelry exudes an atmosphere well in keeping with its 16th century
origins. Panelling, brassware and crackling fires all contribute to a mood of
contentment, well supported in practical terms by splendid food
served either in the convivial bar, where meals are served daily at
lunchtimes and in the evenings, or in the award-winning restaurant
where choice may be made from a mouth-watering à la carte menu.
Sunday roasts are also very popular.

Huggate lies on the Wolds Way and the inn is justly popular with walkers,
whilst historic York and Beverley and their racecourses and the resorts of
Bridlington, Hornsea and Scarborough are within easy reach.

First-rate overnight accommodation is available, all rooms having en suite
facilities, central heating, colour television and tea and coffee tray.

North Yorkshire

Danby

The Fox & Hounds Inn

- Residential 16th Century Coaching Inn set amidst the beautiful North York Moors.
- Freshly prepared dishes served every lunchtime and evening.
- Quality selected wines and Theakston real ales.
- Superb en suite accommodation available.

Special Breaks available November to March. Situated between Castleton and Danby on the Fryup Road.

Ainthorpe, Danby, Whitby, North Yorkshire YO21 2LD
For bookings please Tel: 01287 660218
e-mail: info@foxandhounds-ainthorpe.com
www.foxandhounds–ainthorpe.com

★★★★ INN

Other specialised holiday guides from FHG

PUBS & INNS OF BRITAIN • **COUNTRY HOTELS** OF BRITAIN
WEEKEND & SHORT BREAK HOLIDAYS IN BRITAIN
THE GOLF GUIDE WHERE TO PLAY, WHERE TO STAY
500 GREAT PLACES TO STAY • **SELF-CATERING HOLIDAYS** IN BRITAIN
BED & BREAKFAST STOPS • **CARAVAN & CAMPING HOLIDAYS**
FAMILY BREAKS IN BRITAIN

Published annually: available in all good bookshops or direct from the publisher:
FHG Guides, Abbey Mill Business Centre, Seedhill, Paisley PA1 1TJ
Tel: 0141 887 0428 • Fax: 0141 889 7204
e-mail: admin@fhguides.co.uk • www.holidayguides.com

Argyll & Bute

Ardfern

Highlands

Fort William

Visit the FHG website

www.holidayguides.com

for details of the wide choice of accommodation

featured in the full range of FHG titles

Ratings & Awards

For the first time ever the AA, VisitBritain, VisitScotland, and the Wales Tourist Board will use a single method of assessing and rating serviced accommodation. Irrespective of which organisation inspects an establishment the rating awarded will be the same, using a common set of standards, giving a clear guide of what to expect. The RAC is no longer operating an Hotel inspection and accreditation business.

Accommodation Standards: Star Grading Scheme

Using a scale of 1-5 stars the objective quality ratings give a clear indication of accommodation standard, cleanliness, ambience, hospitality, service and food, This shows the full range of standards suitable for every budget and preference, and allows visitors to distinguish between the quality of accommodation and facilities on offer in different establishments. All types of board and self-catering accommodation are covered, including hotels,
B&Bs, holiday parks, campus accommodation, hostels, caravans and camping, and boats.

VisitBritain and the regional tourist boards, enjoyEngland.com, VisitScotland and VisitWales, and the AA have full details of the grading system on their websites

The more stars, the higher level of quality

★★★★★
exceptional quality, with a degree of luxury

★★★★
excellent standard throughout

★★★
very good level of quality and comfort

★★
good quality, well presented and well run

★
acceptable quality; simple, practical, no frills

National Accessible Scheme

If you have particular mobility, visual or hearing needs, look out for the National Accessible Scheme. You can be confident of finding accommodation or attractions that meet your needs by looking for the following symbols.

 Typically suitable for a person with sufficient mobility to climb a flight of steps but would benefit from fixtures and fittings to aid balance

 Typically suitable for a person with restricted walking ability and for those that may need to use a wheelchair some of the time and can negotiate a maximum of three steps

 Typically suitable for a person who depends on the use of a wheelchair and transfers unaided to and from the wheelchair in a seated position. This person may be an independent traveller

 Typically suitable for a person who depends on the use of a wheelchair in a seated position. This person also requires personal or mechanical assistance (eg carer, hoist).

Family-Friendly Pubs & Inns

This is a selection of establishments which make an extra effort to cater for parents and children. The majority provide a separate children's menu or they may be willing to serve small portions of main course dishes on request; there are often separate outdoor or indoor play areas where the junior members of the family can let off steam while Mum and Dad unwind over a drink.

For details of more properties which welcome children, see the FHG website

www.holidayguides.com

half portions

children's menu

garden or play area

baby-changing facilities

high chairs

family room

THE WELLINGTON ARMS
203 Yorktown Road, Sandhurst,
Berkshire GU47 9BN
Tel: 01252 872408
www.thewellingtonarms.co.uk

VICTORIA INN
Perranuthnoe, Near Penzance,
Cornwall TR20 9NP
Tel: 01736 710309
www.victoriainn-penzance.co.uk

CROOKED INN
Stoketon Cross, Trematon,
Saltash, Cornwall PL12 4RZ
Tel: 01752 848177
www.crooked-inn.co.uk

KINGS ARMS HOTEL
Hawkshead, Ambleside,
Cumbria LA22 0NZ
Tel: 015394 36372
www.kingsarmshawkshead.co.uk

EAGLE & CHILD INN
Kendal Road, Staveley,
Cumbria LA8 9LP
Tel: 01539 821320
www.eaglechildinn.co.uk

MARDALE INN
St Patrick's Well, Bampton,
Cumbria CA19 2RQ
Tel: 01931 713244
www.mardaleinn.co.uk

GILPIN BRIDGE
Bridge End, Levens,
Near Kendal, Cumbria LA8 8EP
Tel: 015395 52206
www.gilpinbridgeinn.co.uk

GREYHOUND HOTEL
Main Street, Shap, Penrith,
Cumbria CA10 3PW
Tel: 01931 716474
www.greyhoundshap.co.uk

QUEEN'S HEAD
Main Street, Hawkshead,
Cumbria LA22 0NS
Tel: 015394 36271
www.queensheadhotel.co.uk

DOLPHIN INN
Kingston, Near Kingsbridge,
Devon TQ7 4QE
Tel: 01548 810314
www.dolphin-inn.co.uk

MALTSTERS ARMS
Bow Creek, Tuckenhay,
Near Totnes, Devon TQ9 7EQ
Tel: 01803 732350
www.tuckenhay.com

THE CRICKETERS
Clavering, Near Saffron Walden,
Essex CB11 4QT
Tel: 01799 550442
www.thecricketers.co.uk

KING'S HEAD INN
Birdwood, Near Huntley,
Gloucestershire GL19 3EF
Tel: 01452 750348
www.kingsheadbirdwood.co.uk

RHYDSPENCE INN

Whitney-on-Wye, Near Hay-on-Wye,
Herefordshire HR3 6EU
Tel: 01497 831262
www.rhydspence-inn.co.uk

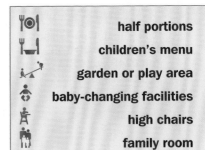

half portions
children's menu
garden or play area
baby-changing facilities
high chairs
family room

SARACENS HEAD INN

Symonds Yat East, Ross-on-Wye,
Herefordshire HR9 6JL
Tel: 01600 890435
www.saracensheadinn.co.uk

CHEQUERS INN

The Street, Smarden,
Near Ashford, Kent TN27 8QA
Tel: 01233 770217
www.thechequerssmarden.com

WHITE HORSE INN

The Street, Boughton,
Kent ME13 9AX
Tel: 01227 751343
www.whitehorsecanterbury.co.uk

WHIPPER-IN HOTEL

Market Place, Oakham,
Leicestershire & Rutland LE15 6DT
Tel: 01572 756971
www.brook-hotels.co.uk

COOK AND BARKER

Newtown-on-the-Moor, Morpeth,
Northumberland NE65 9JY
Tel: 01665 575234
www.cookandbarkerinn.co.uk

TOLLGATE INN

Church Street, Kingham,
Oxfordshire OX7 6YA
Tel: 01608 658389
www.thetollgate.com

THE FLOWER POT

Ferry Lane, Henley-on-Thames,
Oxfordshire RG9 3DG
Tel: 01491 574721

MYTTON AND MERMAID

Atcham, Shrewsbury,
Shropshire SY5 6QG
Tel: 01743 761220
www.myttonandmermaid.co.uk

THE LAMB INN

High Street, Hindon
Wiltshire SP3 6DP
Tel: 01747 820573
www.lambathindon.co.uk

FAIRFAX ARMS

Gilling East, York,
North Yorkshire YO62 4JH
Tel: 01439 788212
www.fairfaxarms.co.uk

CARISBROOKE

Drumduan Road, Forres,
Aberdeen, Banff & Moray IV36 1BS
Tel: 01309 672585
www.carisbrooke-hotel.co.uk

ABERDOUR HOTEL

38 High Street, Aberdour,
Fife KY3 0SW
Tel: 01383 860325
www.aberdourhotel.co.uk

YANN'S AT GLENEARN HOUSE

Perth Road, Crieff,
Perth & Kinross PH7 3EQ
Tel: 01764 650111
www.yannsatglenearnhouse.com

CASTLE VIEW HOTEL

16 Bridge Street, Chepstow,
Monmouthshire NP16 5EZ
Tel: 01291 620349
www.hotelchepstow.co.uk

MUSEUM OF LONDON DOCKLANDS
No1 Warehouse, West India Quay, London E14 4AL
Tel: 0870 444 3855 • e-mail: info@museumoflondon.org.uk
www.museumoflondon.org.uk

·K·U·P·E·R·A·R·D·
READERS'
OFFER
2009

This voucher entitles the bearer to TWO full price adult tickets for the price of ONE on presentation at the Museum of London Docklands admission desk. A max. of one person goes free per voucher. Offer valid until 31 Dec. 2009. Only one voucher per transaction. Non-transferable and non-exchangeable. No cash alternative. Subject to availability. Tickets allow unlimited entry for one year. Children enter free as standard all year round.

NOT TO BE USED IN CONJUNCTION WITH ANY OTHER OFFER

LEIGHTON BUZZARD RAILWAY
Page's Park Station, Billington Road,
Leighton Buzzard, Bedfordshire LU7 4TN
Tel: 01525 373888
e-mail: station@lbngrs.org.uk
www.buzzrail.co.uk

·K·U·P·E·R·A·R·D·
READERS'
OFFER
2009

One FREE adult/child with full-fare adult ticket
Valid 15/3/2009 - 8/11/2009

NOT TO BE USED IN CONJUNCTION WITH ANY OTHER OFFER

BUCKINGHAMSHIRE RAILWAY CENTRE
Quainton Road Station, Quainton,
Aylesbury HP22 4BY
Tel & Fax: 01296 655720
e-mail: bucksrailcentre@btconnect.com
www.bucksrailcentre.org

·K·U·P·E·R·A·R·D·
READERS'
OFFER
2009

One child FREE with each full-paying adult
Not valid for Special Events

NOT TO BE USED IN CONJUNCTION WITH ANY OTHER OFFER

BEKONSCOT MODEL VILLAGE & RAILWAY
Warwick Road, Beaconsfield,
Buckinghamshire HP9 2PL
Tel: 01494 672919
e-mail: info@bekonscot.co.uk
www.bekonscot.com

·K·U·P·E·R·A·R·D·
READERS'
OFFER
2009

One child FREE when accompanied by full-paying adult
Valid February to October 2009

NOT TO BE USED IN CONJUNCTION WITH ANY OTHER OFFER

From Roman settlement to Dockland's regeneration, unlock the history of London's river, port and people in this historic West India Quay warehouse. Discover a wealth of objects, from whalebones to WWII gas masks, in state-of-the-art galleries, including Mudlarks, an interactive area for children; Sailortown, an atmospheric re-creation of 19thC riverside Wapping; and London, Sugar & Slavery, which reveals the city's involvement in the transatlantic slave trade.

Open: daily 10am-6pm. Closed 24-26 December.

Directions: 2 minutes' walk from West India Quay. Nearest Tube Canary Wharf.

FHG GUIDES, ABBEY MILL BUSINESS CENTRE, PAISLEY PA1 1TJ • www.holidayguides.com

---

A 70-minute journey into the lost world of the English narrow gauge light railway. Features historic steam locomotives from many countries.

PETS MUST BE KEPT UNDER CONTROL AND NOT ALLOWED ON TRACKS

Open: Sundays and Bank Holiday weekends 22 March to 25 October. Additional days in summer.

Directions: on south side of Leighton Buzzard. Follow brown signs from town centre or A505/A4146 bypass.

FHG GUIDES, ABBEY MILL BUSINESS CENTRE, PAISLEY PA1 1TJ • www.holidayguides.com

---

A working steam railway centre. Steam train rides, miniature railway rides, large collection of historic preserved steam locomotives, carriages and wagons.

Open: daily April to October 10.30am to 4.30pm. Variable programme - check website or call.

Directions: off A41 Aylesbury to Bicester Road, 6 miles north west of Aylesbury.

FHG GUIDES, ABBEY MILL BUSINESS CENTRE, PAISLEY PA1 1TJ • www.holidayguides.com

---

Be a giant in a magical miniature world of make-believe depicting rural England in the 1930s. "A little piece of history that is forever England."

Open: 10am-5pm daily mid February to end October.

Directions: Junction 16 M25, Junction 2 M40.

FHG GUIDES, ABBEY MILL BUSINESS CENTRE, PAISLEY PA1 1TJ • www.holidayguides.com

THE GRASSIC GIBBON CENTRE

Arbuthnott, Laurencekirk,
Aberdeenshire AB30 1PB
Tel: 01561 361668
e-mail: lgginfo@grassicgibbon.com
www.grassicgibbon.com

READERS' OFFER 2009

TWO for the price of ONE entry to exhibition (based on full adult rate only). Valid during 2009 (not groups)

NOT TO BE USED IN CONJUNCTION WITH ANY OTHER OFFER

SCOTTISH MARITIME MUSEUM

Harbourside, Irvine,
Ayrshire KA12 8QE
Tel: 01294 278283
Fax: 01294 313211
www.scottishmaritimemuseum.org

READERS' OFFER 2009

*TWO for the price of ONE
Valid from April to October 2009*

NOT TO BE USED IN CONJUNCTION WITH ANY OTHER OFFER

DALSCONE FARM FUN

Dalscone Farm, Edinburgh Road,
Dumfries DG1 1SE
Tel: 01387 257546 • Shop: 01387 254445
e-mail: dalscone@btconnect.com
www.dalsconefarm.co.uk

READERS' OFFER 2009

*One FREE adult (16 years+)
Valid during 2009*

NOT TO BE USED IN CONJUNCTION WITH ANY OTHER OFFER

GALLOWAY WILDLIFE CONSERVATION PARK

Lochfergus Plantation, Kirkcudbright,
Dumfries & Galloway DG6 4XX
Tel & Fax: 01557 331645
e-mail: info@gallowaywildlife.co.uk
www.gallowaywildlife.co.uk

READERS' OFFER 2009

*One FREE child or Senior Citizen with two full paying adults.
Valid Feb - Nov 2009 (not Easter weekend and Bank Holidays)*

NOT TO BE USED IN CONJUNCTION WITH ANY OTHER OFFER

Visitor Centre dedicated to the much-loved Scottish writer Lewis Grassic Gibbon. Exhibition, cafe, gift shop. Outdoor children's play area. Disabled access throughout.

Open: daily April to October 10am to 4.30pm. Groups by appointment including evenings.

Directions: on the B967, accessible and signposted from both A90 and A92.

Scotland's seafaring heritage is among the world's richest and you can relive the heyday of Scottish shipping at the Maritime Museum.

Open: 1st April to 31st October - 10am-5pm

Directions: situated on Irvine harbourside and only a 10 minute walk from Irvine train station.

Indoor adventure play area, farm park, toyshop and cafe. A great day out for all the family, with sledge and zip slides, mini-golf, trampolines, bumper boats, pottery painting and so much more.

Open: Monday to Saturday 10am-5.30pm.

Directions: just off the A75/A701 roundabout heading for Moffat and Edinburgh.

The wild animal conservation centre of Southern Scotland. A varied collection of over 150 animals from all over the world can be seen within natural woodland settings. Picnic areas, cafe/gift shop, outdoor play area, woodland walks, close animal encounters.

Open: 10am to dusk 1st February to 30 November.

Directions: follow brown tourist signs from A75; one mile from Kirkcudbright on the B727.

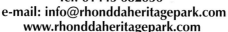
Please note

All the information in this book is given in good faith in the belief that it is correct. However, the publishers cannot guarantee the facts given in these pages, neither are they responsible for changes in policy, ownership or terms that may take place after the date of going to press. Readers should always satisfy themselves that the facilities they require are available and that the terms, if quoted, still apply.

A 60-minute ride along the shores of beautiful Padarn Lake behind a quaint historic steam engine. Magnificent views of the mountains from lakeside picnic spots.

DOGS MUST BE KEPT ON LEAD AT ALL TIMES ON TRAIN

Open: most days Easter to October. Free timetable leaflet on request.

Directions: just off A4086 Caernarfon to Capel Curig road at Llanberis; follow 'Country Park' signs.

Journey through the lanes of cycle history and see bicycles from Boneshakers and Penny Farthings up to modern Raleigh cycles. Over 250 machines on display

PETS MUST BE KEPT ON LEADS

Open: 1st March to 1st November daily 10am onwards.

Directions: brown signs to car park. Town centre attraction.

Make a pit stop whatever the weather! Join an ex-miner on a tour of discovery, ride the cage to pit bottom and take a thrilling ride back to the surface. Multi-media presentations, period village street, children's adventure play area, restaurant and gift shop. Disabled access with assistance.

Open: Open daily 10am to 6pm (last tour 4pm). Closed Mondays Oct - Easter, also Dec 25th to early Jan.

Directions: Exit Junction 32 M4, signposted from A470 Pontypridd. Trehafod is located between Pontypridd and Porth.

Looking for holiday accommodation?

for details of hundreds of properties throughout the UK visit:

www.holidayguides.com

Index of Towns and Counties

Other FHG titles for 2009

FHG Guides Ltd have a large range of attractive
oliday accommodation guides for all kinds of holiday opportunities throughout Britain.
They also make useful gifts at any time of year.
ur guides are available in most bookshops and larger newsagents but we will be happy
to post you a copy direct if you have any difficulty. POST FREE for addresses in the UK.
We will also post abroad but have to charge separately for post or freight.

£9.99

The Original Pets Welcome!
• The bestselling guide to holidays
for pets and their owners

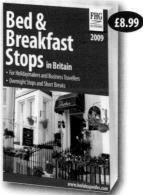

£8.99

Bed & Breakfast Stops
in Britain
• For holidaymakers and business
travellers
• Overnight stops and Short
Breaks

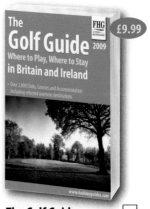

£9.99

The Golf Guide
Where to play, Where to stay.
• Over 2800 golf courses in Britain
with convenient accommodation.
• Holiday Golf in France, Portugal,
Spain, USA and Thailand.

£7.99

Pubs & Inns
of Britain
• Including Dog-friendly Pubs
• Accommodation, food and
traditional good cheer

£6.99

Country Hotels
of Britain
• Hotels with Conference,
Leisure and Wedding Facilities

£7.99

Caravan & Camping Holidays
in Britain
• Campsites and Caravan parks
• Facilities fully listed

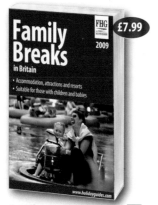

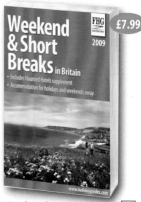

Family Breaks ☐
in Britain
• Accommodation, attractions and resorts
• Suitable for those with children and babies

Self-Catering Holidays ☐
in Britain
• Cottages, farms, apartments and chalets
• Over 400 places to stay

Weekend & Short Breaks ☐
in Britain
• Accommodation for holidays and weekends away

Tick your choice above and send your order and payment to

**FHG Guides Ltd. Abbey Mill Business Centre
Seedhill, Paisley, Scotland PA1 1TJ
TEL: 0141- 887 0428 • FAX: 0141- 889 7204
e-mail: admin@fhguides.co.uk**

FHG
K·U·P·E·R·A·R·D

Deduct 10% for 2/3 titles or copies; 20% for 4 or more.

Send to: NAME ....

ADDRESS ....

....

....

POST CODE ....

I enclose Cheque/Postal Order for £ ....

SIGNATURE ....DATE ....

Please complete the following to help us improve the service we provide.
How did you find out about our guides?:

☐ Press   ☐ Magazines   ☐ TV/Radio   ☐ Family/Friend   ☐ Other